Working the Bench

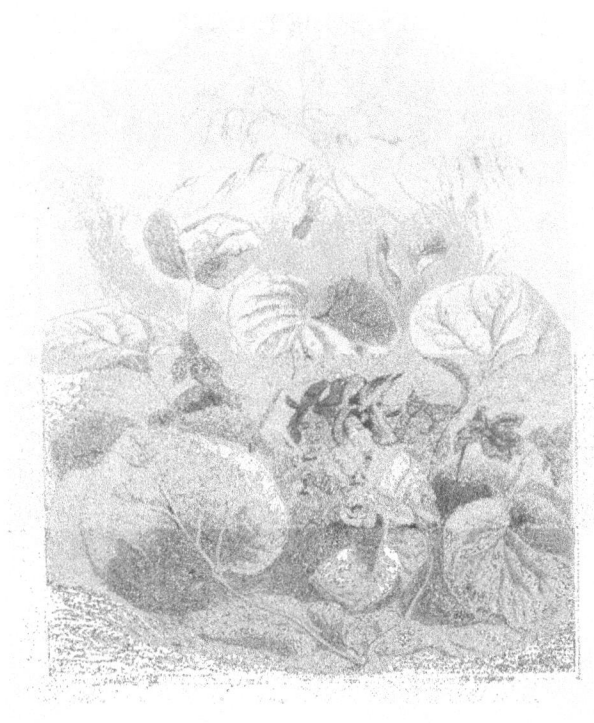

Working the Bench

A Practical Guide to

Natural Botanical Perfumery

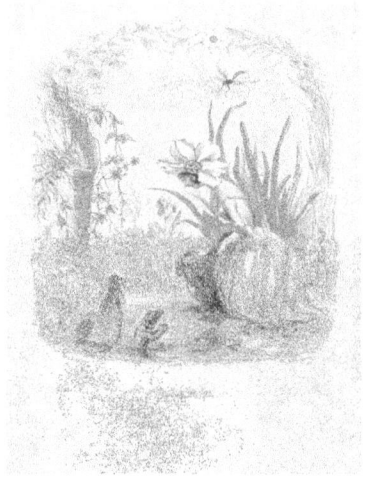

By Justine M Crane

ISBN-13:978-1478150213

ISBN-10:1478150211

Designed and typeset by Justine M Crane

Manufactured in the U.S.A.

Why do we shed the rose's bloom

Upon the cold insensate tomb?

. . . I ask no balm to steep

With fragrant tears my bed of sleep;

But now while every pulse is glowing,

Let me breathe the balsam flowing.

ANACREON

FORWARD

With its poetic beginning Working the Bench A Practical Guide is altogether a gentle and seductive invitation into the world of botanical perfumery.

It is easy to detect Justine Crane's tangible passion for the subject as she takes you back through the rich history some 4,000 years. There is a distinct sense from the start of the workbook that perfume creation is something mystical and highly skilled, letting you know in no uncertain terms that the work and practical instruction therein is not for the half- hearted or the lazy.

Working the Bench A Practical Guide is filled to the brim with gems of information and reliable trusted content, covering all angles from safety, procuring raw materials, care of equipment and tools to detailed instruction on composition, perfume types and strengths to practical charts on dilution and evaluations.

It includes a scent vocabulary and seasoned perfumers tips on perfume production, and making tinctures and extracts.
Justine is also an experienced soap maker and she includes a detailed lesson on soap making and butter and balm formulations along with a useful study in making perfumed oils, giving the all-important dilution guidelines.

The real work for the apprentice perfumer is in the study of the detailed trials and essence evaluations and the sheets to complete this work, along with the necessary guidelines, are also contained in the book.

There is a very valuable chapter on base compounds as well as an itemized guide for formulating your masterpieces.
The workbook concludes on an exciting note as it goes into some lengths on setting up your perfumery business and selling your creations & compositions.

As one would expect it contains a complete glossary and sources list at the end.

Ruth Ruane

PREFACE

Working the Bench A Practical Guide has been a work in progress for many years. My hope is that this book will streamline the process of creating natural botanical perfume for the beginning apprentice perfumer in a manner which is concise and professional, and will serve as a treatise based on experience. With an eye toward cutting the confusion of creating perfume, I have compiled the information in this book in an effort to both simplify the process, and attempt to instill passion in the reader for this art form.

ACKNOWLEDGEMENTS

I would like to acknowledge with much gratitude, love and appreciation the information, friendship and graciousness provided to me by Natural Botanical Perfumers and other experts in the field of Natural Botanical Perfumery, most notably Ms. Shelley Waddington, Ms. Amanda Feeley, Ms. Ane Walsh, Ms. Marian del Vecchio, Ms. Ruth Ruane, Ms. Yuko Fukami, Ms. Holly Simpson, and Ms. Lisa Abdul-Quddus.

Special acknowledgements go to Anastasia Angelopolous for being the spark that lit the flame; to Ylva Rubenssen for fanning the flame into an inferno with 'Amulette'; to Tonie Silver for the encouragement that bordered on harassment (but was the kick in the pants necessary to continue on); to Lisa Camasi for being the oracle for all my questions, and for allowing me entrée into the 'inner circle'; to Laurie Stern whose open heart gives me great comfort (she also makes a stunning mean perfume), and last but not least, all the friends, family, vendors, and clients who have stood by me all these years offering encouragement and bolstering my confidence to continue on ~ I thank you all.

INTRODUCTION

Working the Bench began as a workbook for an online perfumery course which I began teaching in 2008. Since then, it has been expanded upon, edited to death, rewritten and edited even more at least a dozen times since its original 40 or so page instructional. I don't claim to present all the answers to creating natural botanical perfume, and I certainly do not claim or promise to make you, the reader, into the world's greatest natural botanical perfumer through this book's instruction, however I do believe this book will provide a good place for a novice to start. You will find gaps in places such as those in the history section wherein the perfume contributions of some countries and cultures have been left out. This was not done maliciously or with any negative intent, I simply have not had the opportunity to study further those cultures and their contributions enough to feel confident to include them here. Any gaps in technique are attributed to gaps in knowledge – I don't perform certain formulation techniques other perfumers may perform, so I did not include any techniques, 'secrets', or tips within the pages of this book that I haven't tried with success. As stated previously, *Working the Bench* is a good place to start.

CONTENTS

CHAPTER 1 ~ In the Beginning

CHAPTER 2 ~ The Era of Modern Synthetic Perfumery

CHAPTER 1

In the Beginning . . .

"Bring, oh bring the essence pot!
Amber, musk and bergamot,
Eau de Chipre, Eau de Luce,
Sanspareil, and citron juice."
                    Unknown poet

Perfume has a history as long and as rich as the history of mankind itself. Greek legend attributes the first use of perfume to the goddess of love, Venus, and it was to the nymph, Aeonone, upon whom blame is placed for passing the knowledge of perfume to human beings. Thus our passionate love of scent began.

In March of 2007, the National Geographic News reported the discovery of one of the world's oldest perfumeries on Aphrodite's Island (Cyprus). Discovered in 2003 by archaeologists, the perfumery dates back more than 4,000 years. Analysis of the contents of some of the perfume jars held essences which grew in the local region, some which are used today in modern perfumery ~ parsley, coriander, bergamot, pine, and anise. These perfumes were made in a base of oils, primarily olive, and kept in alabaster and clay jars, their contents dabbed upon or rubbed into the skin. Other oils used to create these antiquarian perfumes were oils of ben, sesame, and almond.

The Persian Kings and their courts were famous for their indulgent use of perfumes and cosmetics. The Greek historian, Stabon, wrote that the men of this culture wore so much kohl around their eyes and paint upon their faces that they resembled women. Persians were well known by contemporaries of their time for the extensive use of scented bathing waters and fragrant cleansing creams. Rose, the king of all perfumery ingredients, is a native Persian flower.

The Ancient Egyptians were adept at perfume creation, however, what they created and called perfume was entirely different from what we consider perfume today. Egyptians saw perfume and perfume making as a high art and a religious sacrament, one in which only those entrusted with the secret knowledge of the gods were allowed to possess. Kyphi, the sacred perfume of the Egyptians, was carefully created over many days, the ingredients hand ground to powder and blended together in huge copper bowls, while priests chanted and read prayers from sacred texts – this process of singing and infusing a creative work of art with spiritual vibration is prevalent in nearly all cultures throughout history, and even today is considered a method of raising the spiritual energy in an inanimate object.

Kyphi was believed to be the "sweat of the gods", and as such, its creation was shrouded in mystery. Recipes and formulations for the reproduction of this perfume/incense are still in circulation today. According to the *De Materia Medica* written by Dioscorides, Kyphi was also an important medication. Made with a combination of finely macerated raisins, wine, tree resins, herbs, grasses, woods and honey, this type of perfume was dedicated to use of a spiritual nature in burning, and often eaten to relieve 'ill humours'. It was left to the physicians, alchemists and priests of the time to provide this much lauded perfume. Other more commonly used aromatics in perfumery during this time, according to Dioscorides treaty, were obtained from the white lily, narcissus, rose, jasmine (sambac and grandiflorum), henna flowers, spikenard, iris (orris root), calamus, myrrh, galbanum, cardamom, saffron, Judea balsam, frankincense, cinnamon, fenugreek, galbanum and labdanum.

Modern Kyphi Formulation

To create a kyphi which embodies the spiritual energy necessary for its ritual work, each raw material should be acquired in its whole form and hand ground in a mortar. The recipe provided here is a modern version of kyphi and the quantities have been greatly reduced from what the Ancient Egyptians would have used.

Begin with grinding 7 grams of benzoin resin, 10 grams of calamus root; 10 grams mastic; 10 grams pinon pine resin; 14 grams camphor wood or crystals (wood is preferable but nearly impossible to find); 10 grams light copal resin; 10 grams sandalwood chips; 10 grams tragacanth; 10 grams cinnamon ~ mix together and set aside. Next grind 54 grams juniper berries; 27 grams galbanum resin, and 27 grams orris root. Add all the ground material to a large bowl and pour in 1 – 2 cups of red wine and allow the mixture to set for 24 hours, and then pour off as much of the wine as possible. In another bowl soak 121 grams of dried fruit (traditionally raisins) with 151 grams of fruit wine or juice until the fruit is plump and thoroughly soaked through. Pour off all of the wine/juice, squeezing out any fluid the fruit may have soaked up, and macerate the dried fruit until it is smooth. In a bain marie mix together 121 grams of powdered frankincense resin, 303 grams of honey, and 91 grams of powdered pine resin and heat at medium low for a few hours until the resins are completely melted and the mixture has slightly reduced. While the honey/frankincense/pine mixture is still warm, pour it into the bowl containing the macerated dried fruit, mix well. Add the contents of the honey/dried fruit bowl to the bowl of wine soaked materials and mix well. Finally, once all the ingredients are blended together, add 115 grams of powdered myrrh resin and mix well. Allow the mixture to rest for a few days, then begin rolling the paste into balls or cones and allow those to dry for a few weeks. If the kyphi is too wet or doesn't hold its shape well, roll the kyphi balls/cones into a mixture of orris and sandalwood powder. Burn the kyphi in the evening on charcoal or an incense diffuser.

Queen Cleopatra was the final Pharaoh of Egypt, and perhaps the most famous. Her ambitions lead her to the pinnacle of power as the consort of the Roman Emperor, Caesar. Cleopatra frequently layered the floors of her banquet halls and boudoir with rose petals a foot deep, held down with fine netting upon which her guests walked, and with each step, the scent of roses was released into the air. After Caesar's assassination, Cleopatra set her sights on Marc Antony, using scent to achieve her purpose. Cleopatra soaked the sails of her royal barge in scent when she sailed out to meet with Antony, and she anointed the walls of her parlors with aromatic oils prior to receiving him in her bed.

"Burn'd on the water; -- the poop was beaten gold; purple the sails, and so perfumed, that the winds were love-sick with them" Shakespeare, *Antony and Cleopatra (II.2.192-206)*

The Ancient Greeks were also quite fond of perfume. At one point in Greek history, perfume was supposedly as valuable as food. There is no doubt Greek aristocrats loved perfume and used it often, applying it liberally to the wings of doves and letting them loose in their banqueting halls so perfume would shower down upon the guests.

There may be a conscious connection within the Greek mind at this time of perfume's ability to enhance or change mood. This would harken the first purposeful use of aromatherapy. The Greeks invented perfumes for all possible ailments, as perfume was used as a medicament and curative. The first indication that there were volatile aromatic oils within flowers was discovered by the Greek botanist, Theophrastus, born 370BC. Without doubt, this discovery pushed perfumery to its next, more luxurious level. In her book *Worlds of Sense: Exploring the Senses in History and Across Cultures* by Constance Classen, she writes, "The Greeks, for instance, were such avid connoisseurs of fragrance that they sometimes applied different scents to different parts of the body. The poet Antiphanes writes of the toilet of a wealthy man:

*He bathes in a large gilded tub, and steeps his feet
And legs in rich Egyptian unguent.
His jaws and breasts he rubs with thick palm oil
And both his arms with extract sweet of mint;
His eyebrows and his hair with marjoram
His knees and neck with essence of ground thyme."*

~ 4 ~

Ancient Rome is famous for its indulgent bathing rituals. In every country and culture they invaded, they brought with them the high art of bathing. The Romans built communal bathing *clubs* that also served as gymnasiums and settings for prostitution. Bath houses were called *thermae* and they were owned by the Roman government. Thermae were large buildings and complexes which spanned acres of city property, a testament to their importance in this society. A typical bathing experience would begin with a rub down in oil followed by skin scraping using a tool called a *strigil*, a curved metal knife with a dull blade. A dip in the *tepidarium*, the warm bath, would be followed by a trip to the *caldarium*, the hot bath. Another dip in the tepidarium might follow the trip in the caldarium to help slowly cool the body before immersion in the *frigidarium*, the ice water bath. This dipping and immersing in varying water temperatures would be finished off with a massage of perfumed oils. To Romans, bathing was a social event. Private baths were available, and most wealthy Romans had a small private bath in their home, but the public baths were a place where men conducted business, wound down from a stressful day, or found companionship for the evening.

If the Greeks were indulgent in their use of perfumes, Romans were hyper-indulgent. Nero purchased and burned on a single occasion, and at his country's expense, more incense than his suppliers, all of Arabia, produced in a year. Rome ruled most of the civilized world at this time, and had easy access to rare and costly perfume ingredients. Much like today, expensive and extravagant perfumes were a luxury.

The spread of perfume's use through the ancient world was implemented by the trade in spices. The famous Silk & Spice Trade Routes, originating in China and spreading toward the Middle East to Southern Europe, cut through countries and cultures vastly different from one another. Trade in items necessary to the production of perfume was highly regarded. There was musk from the musk deer living in the mountains of the Himalayas, ambergris washed upon the shores of exotic tropical islands, and rare sandalwood, cut and powdered in the forests of southern India. The far-reaching, world-wide trade in spices and aromatic goods began around 500BC; supplying ancient civilizations with perfumery items they were unable to produce in their own countries.

After the fall of the Roman Empire, and prior to the Crusades, which began in 1099, it appeared that the use of perfume in Europe diminished. This, however, is not true. The Silk and Spice Trade Routes which had been pouring goods, including perfumery items, into Europe from the Orient and Middle East for hundreds of years, continued to do so off and on for centuries. By the 1700's most countries, Portugal in particular, had firmly established trade with China and the Middle East via sea routes to ensure an abundant steady supply of goods.

The Middle East was the hub of education, medicine, art, alchemy and perfumery. Avicenna, Abū Alī Sīnā, a physician and philosopher born in 981BC, is credited with inventing a more effective method of distillation, a process that has undeniably changed the face of perfumery. Through his newly invented process of utilizing a cooling coil in distillation, Avicenna was able to create alcohol in purer form by distilling wine. He also was able to create better quality essential oils. Avicenna distilled rose oil and used it as an antiseptic. There is a rather gruesome account of Avicenna using rose essential oil on an open head wound in which brain matter was exposed, and modern science has proven that rose oil does indeed possess mild antiseptic properties.

During the Middle Ages, it was observed that those who worked with aromatics, the perfumers, alchemists and physicians, appeared immune to most common diseases of the day. One famous perfume/medicine of the dawning Renaissance was called Four Thieves Remedy, named for four grave robbers who murdered, stole and looted from the dying during an outbreak of the Black Plague in Toulouse, France in the mid 1600's. Quoting Dr. Jean Valnet, a famous French aromatherapist, *"During the Great Plague, four robbers were convicted of going to the house of plague victims, strangling them in their beds and then looting their dwellings. For this, they were condemned to be burned at the stake, and in order to have their sentence mitigated, they revealed their secret preservative, after which they were hanged."* The four thieves claimed that a combination of herbs and camphor, which they tied into rags held over their faces, prevented them from becoming ill in the face of the virulent spread of plague.

The first alcohol-based perfume may have been created as early as the 14th century. There is a dubious accounting that the first alcohol based perfume was presented to King Charles V of France in 1375 by

Carmelite nuns. It was made using rectified spirits of wine (distilled wine), lemon balm (melissa), lemon peel, nutmeg and coriander seeds, clove buds, cinnamon and angelica, and was either steeped or re-distilled to produce the final product. Carmelite Water was used as a medicinal tonic as well as for scent. Another accounting states that the first alcohol-based perfume was presented to Queen Elizabeth of Hungary and was made in a base of brandy to which rosemary and other aromatic herbs were added.

A recipe for Queen Elizabeth's Hungary Water exists in the publication *A Woman Beautiful*, c. 1899:

> *Oil of Rosemary ½ oz*
> *Oil of Lavender 2 drahms*
> *Oil of Petitgrain 30 drops*
> *Tincture of Tolu 4 drahms*
> *Orange flower water ½ pint*
> *Spirits of Wine (rectified) 1 ½ pints*

Renaissance Europe and France in particular, were saturated in perfume. King Charles VIII was fond of a perfume made with roses, orange blossoms and rosemary herb, and encouraged his court to use perfumes. These were simple compositions which utilized more flower essences than ever before in history. Catherine de Medici, the Queen and wife to French King, Henry II, was an avid user of perfume. Not only was Catherine credited with introducing French high society to the common use of perfumes, she also introduced high-heels and corsets. Rene de Florentin was Catherine's perfumer, but he may have also provided her with poisons which she used to subdue her enemies. One famous legend attributes the invention of scented gloves to Queen Catherine. The legend states she used these gloves, made by her perfumer alchemist, as gifts to her enemies. Hidden amongst the folds of the gloves were deadly poisons which would seep into the wearer's skin and end their lives. The truth of the scented gloves' origin, however, may be much less nefarious. Catherine was not fond of the smell of the cured leather, so her perfumer imbued her opera gloves with scent to cover the offensive smell. During this period, Grasse, France was the hub of glove

In the book, *Elixirs of Nostradamus*, there is a composition for the making of "aromatic oil", which is used to "warm the womb of an unfruitful woman" and a man "if he is old, past his prime and of little use, for it will warm him as well, without adversely affecting his prowess". This seems to be a perfume of medicinal and seductive purposes, and is composed as directed below:

Take about 12 ounces of occidental grey amber (do not be off put by the fact that you need so much, for the child which it will bear will delight you so much it will more than repay you), round about four ounces of best oriental musk, which is red in color, half a pound of finely crushed cloves, four ounces of the inner bark of the best cinnamon, two ounces of Florentine violet roots, one ounce of spikenard and half a pound of the most delicate wild olive wood. Mix all these ingredients carefully and pulverize them. Put the mixture into a small retort, whether you wish to make a lot or a little, and place it inside a pot or earthenware vessel in which you have previously placed sifted ashes. Bury the retort up to its neck and heat an oven made for the purpose. When the oven is properly dry, put the cooking vessel inside it and seal it with well-mixed lime. Now get the fire going underneath it so that it starts off gently but is going more vigorously towards the end. Keep it going until all the precipitation has stopped and you will be able to differentiate between three or four different substances. First to be exuded will be a black oil of such a lively, exquisite and sharp perfume that it is impossible to find any water, or natural or artificial balsam to compare with it. When you have almost come to the end, make up a good strong fire, but not too fierce, not because it would damage the perfume or detract from it, but because the residue left at the bottom when nothing more is coming out is just as highly prized as the oil. For out of it you can make aromatic powders, balls, paternoster beads or other compositions fit for kings and other great princes and lords. When you are halfway through the process, however, change the cooking vessel if you think it would be a good idea, but if you do not, draw the oil off at once. If, on the other hand, you do not want to distil it through a retort, do so through a small glass phial which is only half full when all the ingredients have been put into it, so that it does not overflow while being boiled. Distil it until nothing remains except the pot, which will have as powerful a scent as the oil and be even more pungent, so that you can fumigate gloves in it or make a regal odour, with which none may easily compare.

making, and the movement to scent leather garments, from gloves to vests to belts, brought about the perfume industry there.

Grasse was famous as a village of tanners who specialized in treating and dying goat skin for the glove industry. While visiting Grasse and the area of Provence, Catherine de Medici noticed that the plant life grew in abundance, due to its unique microclimate. She established a workshop and hired Tombarelli, a Florentine chemist, to distill the local plant life for their essential oils, and he created perfumes from the region's bounty. Thus the perfume industry of France was born.

Josephine and Napoleon are credited with reviving the high art of both fashion and fragrance after the French Revolution. Armand-Gustave Houbigant was assigned as Josephine's personal perfumer in 1807. Houbigant created lush and rich floral perfumes which suited Josephine's more exotic island tastes, while Napoleon preferred the lighter, less intrusive scent of citrus and herbs created by Jean Marie Joseph Farina of *Eau de Cologne* fame.

To illustrate Napoleon's particular olfactory tastes, at the end of one of his campaigns, he is reported to have written to Josephine that he was due home to Paris and that she was not to bathe before he returned. There seems to be some unusual overlap in ideologies of cleanliness here as both he and Josephine were known to take long hot baths daily. The instruction not to bathe may lend some credence to modern studies in human pheromones and their ability to attract sexual partners.

Historical perfumery ingredients during this period and up to the age of modern synthetic perfumery include:

Rose ~ Rose oils were the most desired and significant of perfumery materials, as they are today. The types used most often in antiquarian perfumery were the rosa centifolia, which included the cabbage rose, rose de mai (or May rose), Indian rose and the Moroccan rose, and were typified by their pink petals, and the rosa damascena, which included the Bulgarian rose, Turkish and Moroccan rose, and were typified by their red petals. Roses currently being used in NBP*, in addition to those listed above, are the rosa odorata (tea rose), rosa rugosa of Chinese origin, and rosa bourbonia (also a centifolia). Rose oils can be obtained in essential oil form (hydro distilled), or in concrete and absolute form (solvent extracted). According to *The Complete Guide to the Use of Oils in Aromatherapy and Herbalism* by Julia Lawless, "the damask rose, on account of its fragrance, belongs to cephalics . . . oil of roses is used by itself to cool hot inflammations or swellings, and to bind and stay fluxes of humours to sores." Rose oil and rose floral waters were part of the medica, used for hundreds of ailments, from digestive and menstrual issues, to fever and skin problems. Rose oils are rare and costly and add a lushness and fullness to a fragrance that is unobtainable with any other perfume material.

Jasmine ~ Jasmine oils were obtained through enfleurage by placing the delicate blossoms one by one onto panes of screening or glass covered with purified fat. The pomade, the result of enfleurage, was then washed with alcohol to obtain the "absolute". Nearly all antiquarian perfumers used copious amounts of jasmine in their compositions. Today, jasmine is extracted by use of solvents. Jasmine is one of the more costly perfumery oils, one ounce of jasmine grandiflorum, the more lush and dark of the two main jasmine oils will set one back about $120 USD; jasmine sambac, the sweet night blooming jasmine, is a bit more costly at $135 USD per ounce. Up to 80% of *modern* perfumes contain jasmine oil.

Lavender ~ In antiquarian perfumery, lavender was used copiously, as it was easily grown and its scent easily extracted via steam distillation and oil maceration. The rushes of many a Medieval home were interspersed with lavender and other highly fragrant herbs such as rosemary and balm. There are many varieties of lavender, from the rustic and agrestic types, the bitter herbaceous, to the sweet floral types. Lavenders are used primarily in fougere perfumes, blended with mosses and coumarin (tonka) to give a fern-like quality to perfume. Many men's perfumes are made with lavender.

Frankincense ~ Luban, olibanum, incense, frankincense is one of the greatest, and perhaps oldest, perfumery ingredients known to man. Frankincense has been used throughout history to perfume rooms as a fumigant against insects and disease, as a cover for disagreeable odors, and more importantly, to burn in homage to ancient gods. It was used in the embalming of Egypt's pharaohs, burned during funerary rites, and is a common scent detected upon stepping into nearly any Catholic church today. It was also commonly used in unguents and cosmetics to help beautify skin and maintain the youthfulness of the women, and men, who used them. Frankincense was also an important medicine, having the ability to slow the bleeding of wounds, aid in wound healing, and as a topical antiseptic. Frankincense, grown in the dry, arid regions of Arabia and Africa, was a common commodity carried across the Silk and Spice Trade Routes. According to Trygve Harris of *Enfleurage* in New York City, a modern frankincense expert, the best frankincense is the rare and costly Omani variety. Frankincense is part of the *Burseraceae* family, and grows as a gnarled, wind-bent tree. Frankincense trees can live for hundreds of years. The resin is harvested by cutting the bark and allowing the sap of the tree to ooze out and solidify. Typically frankincense has a bitter, lemony essence, with a warm, clean, resinous dry down. Different varieties possess different levels of these scent elements, and because of its across-the-accords scent profile, it can be used anywhere in a perfume, from a head note, a heart note, a base note, as a bridge, modifier, sacrificial or a fixative.

Myrrh ~ Myrrh was used extensively in unguents, creams and other cosmetics due to its healing and anti-aging properties. Much like frankincense, myrrh was highly sought after, but its cost was nearly three times that of frankincense. In ancient times, a gift of myrrh was as good as gold, as illustrated in the bible. Myrrh was used in much the same way as frankincense; in embalming, fumigation, and perfumery and in medicines. Its growing region mirrors that of frankincense, spreading across the dry, arid regions of Arabia, and is harvested the same way as frankincense; cutting the bark and waiting for tears to form. Myrrh's scent is warm, balsamic, and almost rubbery, with great tenacity. Ovid wrote of the legend of Myrrha in his work, *Metamorphoses*. Myrrha was a princess, a daughter of Cinyras, King of Cyprus, who fell madly in lust with her own father, as the legend goes, and as her punishment for this sin against mankind, she was turned into the myrrh tree, her resinous tears forever running down her brittle branches.

Tuberose ~ Sweet, honey-like, creamy, lush, with jasmine and orange blossom notes, tuberose was another important floral in perfumery, used in higher-end, classic perfumes, and exclusively obtained through enfleurage. Tuberose was used in Victorian times as a funerary flower, and in the tropical islands as a lei or hair ornament. Modern techniques (solvent extraction) are used to obtain tuberose absolutes today. Tuberose is native to Mexico and other Central American countries, and was brought to Europe during the late 1500's by Spanish and Portuguese explorers. Today, tuberose is grown for the perfume industry in France, China, Egypt and Morocco.

Neroli ~ Neroli oil is, and was, obtained through the steam distillation of the bitter orange blossom. It differs from orange blossom absolute/concrete in its method of extraction (orange blossom was extracted through enfleurage/alcohol wash, but is now solvent extracted), and its scent profile. Neroli possesses a cleaner, crisper, less of the blossom and more of the entire bitter orange tree essence, a much more floral version of petit grain, while orange blossom absolute/concrete smells of a blossoming grove of orange trees, heady, narcotic and more like the white floral of gardenia, jasmine and tuberose. Neroli was named after Anne-Marie de la Tremouille de Noirmontier, Princess of Nerola, who, it is historically written, adored the scent of steam distilled bitter orange blossoms. Neroli's historic contribution to perfumery is legion, heralding in the era of colognes, and was used in such popular scents as the original *Eau de Cologne*, and *4711*. Neroli has a light, sweet, floral/petit grain essence of some tenacity.

Citrus & Petit Grain ~ Citrus oils of all types have been used throughout history. The oils of orange, lemon, lime, bergamot and grapefruit are necessary and common ingredients to nearly any perfume. Traditional cologne is not cologne without citrus oils, and many historic, blended perfumes contained bergamot as a top note as it blends well with nearly every other essence, and it has a distinguishing floral characteristic lacking in other citrus oils. Citrus oils are typically cold-pressed, though some are steam-distilled. Petit grain is distilled from the leaves and twigs, and sometimes with the inclusion of flowers, of the bitter orange citrus tree, and is commonly used to adulterate neroli as some varieties contain fewer terpenes (they're the distinguishing chemicals that makes citrus smell distinctively *citrusy*). Petit grain oil on its own is sweet and somewhat floral with "green" and citrus notes. Petit grain oils today are derived from many different citrus trees, including lemon, grapefruit, mandarin, lime and combava, as well as orange varieties.

Civet, Musk & Ambergris (Ambra) ~ these three animal derived perfumery materials were highly prized among perfumers for their perceived ability to extend the scent life of their perfume compositions. It has been written that so much musk and civet were used in perfume compositions, that at some point, it was all that could be detected. In William Shakespeare's play, *As You Like It*, the character Touchstone says, *"Civet is of a baser birth than tar, the very uncleanly flux of a cat."* Musk and civet possess very strong animalic, fur-like scents, with notes of indoles and skatoles (especially in civet). Ambergris, however, is a more "silent" attractor, not having as an overt or noxious scent as civet and musk, but possessing a seaweed-like scent with undertones of warm human skin, and just a very, very light essence of bad breath. It has the distinction of rounding out and warming a formulation, as well as exalting a perfume. Castoreum from beaver was also used, as well as musk from American musk rats, but to a lesser degree than the other animal derived essences. Currently, ethical perfumers use cruelty-free animal derived substances such as hyracium (African Stone) from fossilized hyrax excrement, and tinctures and evulsions from domesticated farm animals, such as goat hair tincture from goats, and horse chestnut or horse sweat/hair tincture from horses. In some cases, extractions of cheese are utilized to give a perfume a certain animalic funk.

Orris ~ Orris root, the roots of the plant *Iris Pallida*, are the source of the irone rich, sweet, floral, tenacious and sometimes sensitizing oil of orris/iris. Orris roots must be aged for a period of 3-5 years before their scent can be extracted, historically via oil maceration or alcohol extraction. Today, orris is extracted by volatile solvents or CO_2 extraction to create orris oils and orris "butters". Orris possesses the delicate, sweet and highly sought after essence of violet flowers. Blended with violet leaf absolute, boronia, and a few other choice floral aromatics, a close approximation of a violet flower perfume can be created. Orris is an excellent fixative. Historically, orris was also used in powder form to scent the body, and the whole root as a teething ring for babies.

Benzoin ~ Used primarily as a fixative, benzoin's sweet, resinous, vanilla-like essence has been prized by perfumers for thousands of years, and was just as important to ancient perfume rituals as was frankincense and myrrh. Benzoin has been used in all aspects of perfumery, from its inception as an aromatic burnt as incense, to the height of perfumery when everything imaginable was scented, from gloves, belts, hats, entire costumes, to paper and ornamentals. Benzoin is an excellent fixative in small amounts, helping to extend the length of time a perfume lingers on the skin without adversely scenting the composition. Certain forms of benzoin are sensitizers.

Scented gloves, artificial flowers and feathers dominated fashion at the very beginning of the era of modern perfumery. During the Belle Epoch, Loïe Fuller, a famous European actress of the time, set the stage for the evolution of the Art Nouveau movement and she inspired perfumers with her art. As an actress, she used as her instruments lighting, gossamer fabrics, ephemera, illusion and unusual sets. She was called "a flower, a wave, a cloud and a jewel, a personification of ethereal beauty". She was also compared to scent in that she was "dynamic, protean, volatile, fluid, undulating and serpentine". She gave certitude that there was drama to perfume, volatility, and an ability to capture perfume's nature through physicality and elaborate illusory tricks.

In Europe, perfumes were created using an abundance of lush, heady florals – jasmine, tuberose, rose and ylang-ylang that were combined with heavy base notes of sandalwood, patchouli, civet, musk and ambergris. Americans were much more conservative during this time, creating perfumes with more delicate fragrances, perfumes of violet, rose and lily-of-the-valley. Europeans, particularly the French, were doused in scent. No self-respecting wealthy Frenchwoman would leave home without first immersing herself in the *parfum du jour*. Perfumes made during this time used more synthetics and isolates than ever before. Through organic chemistry and synthesis, perfumery ingredients like lilac, lily-of-the-valley and gardenia became much more cost effective to the perfumer and the consumer.

CHAPTER 2

The Era of Modern Synthetic Perfumery . . .

The 1890's witnessed the era of modern perfumery, with perfume houses of Guerlain, Houbigant and Caron leading the way. *Fougere Royale* was created by perfumer Paul Parquet for the House of Houbigant in 1882 and was the first modern Fougere perfume (fougere means "fern"). A trend setter, *Fougere Royale* was based around a fresh herbaceous mossy character, with notes of vanilla, musk, hay, carnation, rose, bergamot, lavender and clary sage giving life to an otherwise previously non-existent perfume classification. Fougere's are now one of the most popular perfume classes with perfumes such as *Carrington, Brut, Lapidus pour homme* and *Wild Country* sharing the classification. Fougere's are primarily a men's perfume type, but have recently become a favorite of women. *Jicky* by Guerlain is perhaps one of the more famous perfumes of all time, created by Aimee Guerlain in 1889; Jicky is in the Oriental/Amber family of perfumes with notes of amber, benzoin, vanilla, olibanum, leather, jasmine, orris, rose, rosewood, lemon and bergamot. The story of the perfume's name is shrouded in mystery; in one accounting it is noted that "Jicky" was the name of Aimee Guerlain's English lover, another accounting notes that the name derives from Aimee's nephew, Jacques Guerlain, another later famous perfumer, whose nickname was Jicky. Regardless of which is the true story, the perfume withstood the test of time.

1900's

The house of Houbigant once again introduced a classic in 1912, *Queleques Fleurs*, created by perfumer Robert Bienaimé, a lush floral composition with civet, musk, heliotrope, jasmine, lilac, rose de mai, orange blossom and citrus, and utilizing the trendy synthetic compound, aldehyde C-12 MNA, which creates a lush citrusy, floral, ambery note. Guerlain produced *L'Heure Bleu* at this time, a wildly famous perfume, created by perfumer Jacques "Jicky" Guerlain. *L'Heure Bleu* is a classic of epic stature, highly coveted and dearly loved by perfumistas the world over. *L'Heure Bleu* is a sweet floral with notes of vetyver, cedar, musk, clove bud, jasmine, clary sage, neroli and tarragon. *Narcisse Noir*, another beautiful, classic perfume, created in 1911 by Caron owner and perfumer, Ernest Daltroff, was cutting-edge, in both the gorgeously scented perfume and its luxurious packaging. According to some accountings, Gloria Swanson adored this lush floral perfume with its notes of civet, sandalwood, jasmine, jonquil, narcissus, lemon, petitgrain and orange blossom.

1920's

Francis Coty (real name Francis Sportuno of Corsica) introduced *Emeraude* in 1923, a perfume which can still be purchased today. *Emeraude* was not considered a ground-breaking perfume, but it held high appeal for his target market: women. Part of Coty's legend includes a story relating to the "launch" of Coty's perfume career: According to this story, Coty was attempting to sell a bottle of one of his latest creations (one of dozens he created over his long perfuming career), and was having a difficult time with the manager of the establishment, when he accidentally-on-purpose dropped the bottle of perfume on the floor. What is said to have commenced next is pure perfume fantasy ~ supposedly several customers in the store rushed over to the perfume counter to smell the wonderful fragrance wafting through the air, and asked where they could purchase the perfume. Coty's famous career began in earnest.

Paul Poirot heralded in the age of fashion designer/per fumier with his contribution of *Parfums de Rosine*, the fragrance house, and *Les Ateliers de Martine,* the fashion house. Poirot employed famous perfumer Henri Alméras, who later went on to create *Joy* in 1930 for Jean Patou. Taking up Poirot's lead, many fashion houses began creating perfumes, some of which are still famous today.

Coco Chanel, a hat maker-gone-high-fashion introduced her classic contribution to perfumery, *Chanel No. 5*, in 1921. Created by perfumer Ernest Beaux, a Russian immigrant who had previously worked for the perfume house of Rallet in Moscow, *Chanel No. 5* utilized a higher proportion of aldehydes than any other perfume before, creating a unique scent profile which customers and clients the world over adored. Marilyn Monroe was once asked what she wore to bed and her answer was, in her soft, sultry voice, "Chanel No. 5."

1930's

Joy by the house of Patou, created by perfumer Henri Alméras in 1930, was another avant-garde perfume, and touted as one of the most costly perfumes ever made. Joy utilizes almost no base notes, instead filling its space with lush, decadent florals ~ jasmine, lily of the valley, orchid, rose, ylang-ylang, peach, orris and aldehydes. *Shocking*, introduced in 1937 by couturier, Elsa Shiaparelli, and created by perfumer Jean Amic, a Grasse perfumer for Roure Bertrand Dupont, was yet another exceptional perfume of its time. Ms. Shiaparelli asked that the bottle be designed to look like the silhouette of famous femme fatale, Mae West. The perfume itself was a truly shocking combination of raspberry, tarragon, deep florals, moss and vanilla

Tabu, created by Dana by world-famous perfumer Jean Carles, was yet another stand-out in this era of wild and exotic perfumes. It is said that the brief given for *Tabu* was to create a "whore's perfume", something outrageously erotic and lush, with loads of civet and patchouli, and shored with jasmine, clove bud, narcissus and rose.

1940's

Perfumes in Europe and America boomed in the post-World War II era. An abundance of creative, never-before-seen scents hit the market. *Chantilly* was introduced by Dana, a sweet little darling of a perfume based around tonka, leather, musk, jasmine, rose and fruit notes. One of the more famous contributions came from perfumer Edmond

Roudnitska when he presented the world with *Femme de Rochas*, a gorgeous fruity chypre with lush notes of patchouli and vanilla with amber and benzoin, jasmine, rose de mai, orris, bergamot, cumin, and that lovely aldehyde C14 with its fruity, peachy scent. Femme was commissioned by Marcel Rochas as a gift to his lovely wife, Helene. The bottle is supposedly designed, again, after the curvaceous Mae West. The house of Dior had a very busy decade with the introduction of *Miss Dior* in 1947 (the same year they launched their first major women's fashion line) and *Diorama* in 1949. *Miss Dior* was created by perfumers Jean Carles, Paul Vacher and Serge Heftler Louiche, and was a floral/animalic chypre with notes of vetyver, amber, sandalwood, narcissus, orris, rose, sage, galbanum and heavy aldehydes. Edmond Roudnitska, one of the world's greatest perfumers, created *Diorama*, a beautifully constructed, well-loved perfume of its time, with notes of labdanum, moss, vetyver, patchouli, hydrocitronellal (a muguet/lily-of-the-valley note), jasmine, peachy aldehydes, cumin, cinnamon and nutmeg. *L'Air du Temps* by Nina Ricci, created by perfumer Francis Fabian, was launched in 1948, and was marketed as a virgin's perfume. Light and floral, fresh and young, *L'Air du Temps*, with its trademark doves on the cap, is still a favorite today, made with notes of vetyver, moss, sandalwood, orchid, lily, ylang-ylang, rose de mai, peach and neroli.

1950's

Edmond Roudnitska created another masterpiece for Dior when he formulated *Diorissimo* in 1955, a fresh floral fragrance with notes of civet and sandalwood, jasmine, rose, loads of aldehydes, and bergamot. It seemed a simpler composition than his previous work for Dior, but its impact was significant. Roudnitska was not fond of the gourmand notes a lot of perfumers were using and created *Diorissimo* with fewer components and tended to head in a greener direction. *Cabochard* by Madame Grés, created by perfumer Bernard Chant in 1959 was yet another standout. *Cabochard* is a five-star leather chypre with notes that included castoreum (from beaver or synthetics), musk, patchouli, rose, ylang-ylang, jasmine, geranium, significant aldehydes and fruit notes. Madame Grés' fashion house was famous for creating clothing that was loose and graceful, so *Cabochard* was created to reflect the style. Estée Lauder burst onto the perfume scene in 1953 with her famous *Youth Dew*, originally created as a bath oil to appease the money conscious housewives of post-World War II America. *Youth Dew* was created by perfumers at Ameringen-Haebler, Inc., the predecessor to International Flavors & Fragrances (IFF), a consortium of perfumers and chemists creating both finished perfumes and aromachemicals for use in the perfume industry. *Youth Dew* is a gorgeous amber parfum with sweet floral-spicy notes and softly diffusing aldehydes. Wildly popular among American housewives of the time, *Youth Dew* launched Estée Lauder's lucrative career.

1960's

Fidji, from the house of Guy Laroche, was created by perfumer Josephine Catapano in 1966. A floral/floral with oriental undertones, *Fidji* was made with lush notes of hyacinth, jasmine, orris, rose, carnation, ylang-ylang, lemon, musk, sandalwood and moss. *Fidji* offers its wearer a kiss of tropical bliss and remains quite popular. Paco Rabanne created *Calandre* in 1969, a beautiful aldehydic floral with notes of oakmoss, musk, sandalwood, geranium, jasmine, lily, orris, aldehydes and leafy greens. *Calandre* begins with a heavy hit of aldehydes and green notes, which segue into light florals, and then ends with a sweet, light musky tone.

1970's

Trendy perfumes which echoed the Women's Movement were all the rage in the 1970's. Marketing for perfumes during this period were ratcheted up to a higher degree than ever before, using the cultural boon of newly independent working women as a launching point, and with it, the era of designer perfumes began, with Charles Revson and Yves St. Laurent leading the way. *Charlie*, made by Revlon, the cosmetic giant owned by American entrepreneur, Charles Revson, typifies the scent of the 1970's. *Charlie* owes much of its success to its marketing and low cost ~ Charles Revson was a hard-nosed businessman and perfectionist and spent extensively on ad campaigns, creating captivating television commercials and plastering *Charlie* inside dozens of women's magazines, making *Charlie* the number one selling perfume in the 1970's. *Charlie* wasn't a particularly well-made perfume, smelling rather cheap and one dimensional, but that didn't deter from its popularity. Made with notes of vanilla, musk, cyclamen, rose, lily-of-the-valley, peach, tarragon and hyacinth, *Charlie* charmed an entire generation. *Opium*, however, was an entirely different story. Presented by couturier, Yves St. Laurent, *Opium* represented the mature, sophisticated, sexually unhindered woman of the 70's. *Opium* is a lush spicy oriental with notes of amber, benzoin, musk, vanilla, sandalwood, rose, ylang-ylang, cinnamon, orange, pimento and aldehydes created by perfumer Jean-Louis Sieuzac. Opium had quite the notorious start, catching the attention of American Coalition against Opium and Drug use, as well as the Federal Justice Department, who attempted to have the perfume banned because they felt it was promoting drug use. The original name for this perfume was "Black Orchid", but the perfume house capitalized on the perfume's more disreputable name, making *Opium* one of the most successful perfumes in history. Designer trendsetters of the time included Geoffrey Beene who introduced *Grey Flannel* in 1976; Halston who introduced *Halston* in 1975, *Halston Z14* and *Halston 1-12* in 1976; Oscar de la Renta who introduced *Oscar* in 1977, and Diane von Furstenberg who introduced *Tatiana* in 1975.

Who could forget the iconic *Jean Nate*?

Created in 1935 by Charles of the Ritz, Jean Nate became a cultural icon of scent during the 70's and 80's. Big yellow bottles filled to brimming with bright effervescent alcohol-based colognes were liberally splashed and poured over generations of women, from grandmothers to little girls.

1980's

Giorgio was introduced in 1981 by the house of Giorgio of Beverly Hills. Giorgio is a floral/floral with notes of amber, cedar, sandalwood, gardenia, orchid, tuberose, bergamot, aldehydes with green and fruit notes, and was created by a team of perfumers at Florasynth. Giorgio of Beverly Hills further contributed *Giorgio Beverly Hills* in 1981, *Giorgio for Men* in 1984, and *Giorgio V.I.P.* in 1987. *Beautiful* by Estée Lauder was another great perfume of the 1980's, and remains so today. A sweet, green/floral with great complexity and depth, made with notes of vanilla, frankincense, myrrh, sandalwood, ylang-ylang, orange blossom, clary sage, marigold, lily-of-the-valley and tangerine. *Eternity* by couturier Calvin Klein was created by the great Sophia Grojsman, one of the very best perfumers in the world today. *Eternity* utilized oceanic notes (from synthetics) which seemed to set perfume on a different path. Made with obscure notes called "woody complex" and "citrus complex", and bolstered by musk, rose, jasmine, and leafy green notes, along with that famous aldehydic oceanic note. Despite the oceanic tone of this perfume, it is considered a floral.

1990's

Escape, another Calvin Klein perfume, again utilized the oceanic notes that launched *Eternity,* only this time it was paired with fruit instead of floral, though this perfume is usually classified as a green/floral. This time, instead of a famous perfumer, Klein chose a panel of perfumers at Mane to create this perfume, utilizing notes of apricot, musk, sandalwood, melon, heliotrope, cyclamen and rose. As with *Eternity,* *Escape* became a favorite due to heavy advertising campaigns. The house of Dior again stepped in and presented *Dune* in 1992, created by perfumer Jean-Louise Sieuzac. There is quite a funny story about the launch of this particular perfume ~ because the perfume was to evoke feelings of being on a beach; the launch was set to take place in Biarritz, France, which, to the dismay of the event coordinators, turned out to be a nudist beach. *Dune* is an oriental/amber made with notes of amber, vanilla, patchouli, broom, rose, ylang-ylang, bergamot, rosewood and mandarin. *Poeme* by Lancome was created by perfumer Jacques Cavalier, and presented the newest trend in perfume ~ the nauseatingly sweet, syrupy, fruity/floral. *Poeme* is considered a classic perfume by many, and much like Thierry Mugler's sugary confection *Angel, Poeme* is either loved or detested.

2000's

The jury's still out on what perfume of this decade is a classic ~ perfumes are being launched in their hundreds every year, some falling by the wayside, never to be seen again, along with re-launches of old classics popping up here and there. One thing that must be noted at this point is that most, if not all, classic perfumes of the previous decades have been reformulated to pass the stringent inspection of the International Fragrance Association's implementation of bans and restrictions on natural and synthetic perfumery materials based on human safety concerns, and also with the passage of the Endangered Species Act in 1973 with its ban on the use of endangered animal species in perfumery. New perfumes are carefully created to fall within the guidelines of the IFRA, which leads some to believe that the soul of perfumery has been lost. This wave of reformulation has created a new genre of perfumista – the vintage collector. Pre-1980's perfumes are all the rage, with bottles of vintage and antique perfumes being sold and traded like stocks. The 2000's are dominated by celebrity scents, with Britney Spears launching *Curious* in 2004, and a subsequent perfume every year since; *Fantasy* in 2005, *Curious In Control* and *Midnight Fantasy* in 2006, *Believe* in 2007, *Curious Heart* in 2008, and *Hidden Fantasy* and *Circus Fantasy* in 2009, with silly taglines that read, "Do you dare?", "Everybody has one", "Do you make it hot?", and "What do you have to hide?" Paris Hilton, heiress, has marketed *Paris Hilton, Paris Hilton for men, Just Me, Just Me for men, Heiress, Heir, CanCan, Fairy Dust* and *Siren*. None of these celebrity perfumes are created by the celebrities themselves. The celebrities, or "their people", write a brief, a perfume description, send the brief off to a panel of perfumers employed by one of the big aroma-chemical companies who put a few perfumers on the job creating the perfumes. When the perfumes are complete, they are given for inspection to the client who then chooses their favorite, and that's what goes to market. Needless to say, as popular as some of the celebrity scents are, few, if any, have fallen into the category of a classic perfume.

A Few Notable Releases in the 2000's

More and more perfumes are being launched exclusively by perfume houses such as L'Artisan with their offerings of *Tea for Two, Iris Pallida, Mure et Musc Parfum, Premier Figuier, Havana Vanille, Bois Farine* (with wheat notes), and *Timbuktu*, capitalizing on the skills of world famous perfumers like Bertrand Duchaufour, Evelyn Boulanger, Celine Ellena, Anne Flipo and Olivia Giacobetti; the house of Byredo; the house of Maison Francis Kurkdjian, headed by perfumer Francis Kurkdjian, offering perfumes of opulence and singularity such as *Acqua Universalis* and *Lumièr Noire pour femme;* Narciso Rodriguez, an American fashion designer, creator of *Narciso Rodriguez for Her Eau de Parfum Intense*, released in 2009, and Annick Goutal, with perfumer Isabelle Doyen, creating the classic perfumes *Annick Goutal Songes* and *Mandragore Pourpre.*

Enter the Contemporary Natural Botanical Perfumer

Interest in Natural Botanical Perfumery has been gaining in momentum for decades, however, until the 1990's, they were relatively unknown to the consuming masses, relegated to the dominion of aromatherapy. Thanks to the internet and pioneering Natural Botanical Perfumers, enthusiasm in Natural Botanical Perfumery has reached a pinnacle of success. Some of the earlier NBP pioneers include:

Kathryn Degraff, a photojournalist and world traveler, who studied perfumery and wrote a pivotal article in 1996 about famous perfumer, Edmond Roudnitska

Jeanne Rose, the Grande Dame of Aromatherapy and Natural Botanical Perfumery, former NAHA president, a San Francisco institution, and author, who has written informative and educational books and primers on the art of perfumery since 1972

Francois Michel, a master perfumer of thirty-plus years whose creativity and intuition in the realm of Natural Botanical Perfumery are nothing short of amazing

Christine Malcolm, a thirty-plus year veteran of the NBP world who currently owns and operates Santa Fe Botanical Fragrances, and has received honors in Experimental Psychology for her research in olfactory perception. Ms. Malcolm is a member of the American Society of Perfumers and Women in Flavor and Fragrance in Commerce, and she wrote a chapter in the book *The World of Aromatherapy,* edited by Jeanne Rose and Susan Earle, entitled "Perfumery with Rare Essences".

A Natural Botanical Perfumers' choice of perfumery materials are restricted to those which are, without question, naturally and/or botanically derived, forgoing the use of modern synthetic perfumery materials. Until recently, Natural Botanical Perfumers received very little recognition for their contribution to the art of perfumery, though a growing number of perfumistas and perfume bloggers are currently taking notice, using and reviewing the perfumes of notable Natural Botanical Perfumers, such as *Black Cat* by Laurie Stern of *Velvet & Sweet Pea's Purrfumery, Art Liquide, Vespertina* by Roxana Villa of *Illuminated Perfume, Galatea* by Alexandra Balhoutis of *Strange Invisible Perfumes,* and 2013 FIFI nominee, *Treazon* by Ayala Sender of *Ayala Moriel Perfumes.*

CHAPTER 3

Safety Regards

"Perfumery, as known to most people, is an art, but as known to the expert perfumer, it has become elevated, if not to the level of a science, at least to the level of a scientific art."

Ernest Parry

All ingredients used in a formulation must be researched and determined safe by the perfumer. Check a reputable aromatherapy or essential oil chemistry manual for information regarding issues of allergy, sensitivity, photo toxicity, carcinogenic levels and levels of potential toxicity for each raw material used. The safety manual written by Tisserand and Balac, *Essential Oil Safety: A Guide for Health Care Professionals*, ISBN: 0443052603, is a comprehensive guide to safe use of essential oils.

The IFRA, International Fragrance Association, also provides a comprehensive online data base of restricted and prohibited raw materials. Their website is www.ifraorg.org. The information provided by the IFRA with regard to the potential hazards of some natural materials has been questioned by the Natural Botanical Perfume community.

It has been suggested by Tony Burfield of Cropwatch at www.cropwatch.com that the IFRA has used flawed research data to determine the potential toxicity of some natural raw materials; for example, the IFRA has restricted certain essential oils based on the *lack of information* pertaining to dermal research and analysis, and not on actual facts or findings. However, having pointed out this incongruity, it must be noted that the EU has adopted the IFRA's research and implemented the rulings into the EU Cosmetic Directive, which means anyone creating perfume within the EU must conform to the Directive's rulings. Recent news indicates that the IFRA is "restructuring [their] network aims to achieve efficiencies" through national and regional associates covering North America, Latin America, Europe and Asia-Pacific. What this means is that the IFRA is attempting to regulate perfumery, all forms of perfumery, globally. In order for their directives to work, and possibly hinder the free artistic expression of the perfume communities in the US, Canada, Latin America, and the Asian-Pacific countries, the governmental bodies of each country must adopt them.

What is the International Fragrance Association?

The IFRA website states: "IFRA, the International Fragrance Association, is the official representative body of the fragrance industry worldwide. Its main purpose is to ensure the safety of fragrance materials through a dedicated science program. This focus on fragrance safety helps both the consumer and the environment." **Membership in the IFRA is voluntary, which means the rules and regulations apply only to member of the IFRA or, in most cases, those producing cosmetics and perfumes within the EU.** The IFRA and the RIFM (*Research Institute for Fragrance Materials*) submit their findings on the safety of perfume ingredients to the European Union Cosmetic Directive, who then implement the findings as rules which the cosmetics'/perfume companies within the jurisdiction of the EU must abide. The IFRA is currently attempting to incorporate their regulations into international cosmetics directives, which means at some point other countries, the US in particular, may implement the regulations, and businesses which fall under the definition of "cosmetics", which includes perfumes, will be required to implement them into their formulation practices. The downside of all this regulation, aside from the additional work it places on the small business owner, is that the IFRA often restricts, and even mulls the idea of banning perfume and flavor materials based on their inability to pay to have them properly tested.

To find further information regarding the IFRA and its dedicated science program from the perspective of a skeptic, visit Tony Burfield's website "Cropwatch" at www.cropwatch.org.

Basic Safety for the Natural Botanical Perfumer

The perfumer's safety is of utmost importance. The following is a basic list of rules to follow to ensure safety during perfume making experiments.

*If any raw material, finished perfume or alcohol gets into the eyes, rinse immediately with sterile water and seek medical attention if a reaction occurs. An eye-wash station is optimal.

*Wear gloves and protective clothing (apron, long-sleeved shirt) when handling undiluted raw materials to prevent the materials from coming into direct contact with the skin. Protective eyewear is also recommended.

*Work in a well-ventilated room. While working with a known respiratory sensitizer in its whole, undiluted form, it is recommended that a surgical mask be worn.

*Keep all raw materials safely stored away from pets and children. Materials which are not properly stored pose a higher threat of accidental ingestion and poisoning. Pets and children are at a higher risk of accidental poisoning or sensitization by the materials used in natural & botanical perfume making due to their natural curiosity and inability to recognize the hazards.

*NEVER apply a raw fragrant material to the skin without diluting it first! This is typically how many people become sensitized. If a person becomes sensitized to a material, they will have an adverse reaction each time they work with that material.

*NEVER apply a diluted fragrant material on broken or irritated skin as this can cause serious adverse effects such as contact irritation and/or sensitization.

Adverse Reactions:

Phototoxicity – Phototoxic reactions manifest when fragrance materials on the skin are exposed to direct sunlight (heat and light), and is a result of an overheating between a chemical, for example, psoralens and furanocoumarins in essential oils, and ultraviolet light. The results can range from a mild reaction that appears (looks) like sunburn, to a severe blistering rash, brown spots, and can even cause permanent scarring. People with a history of skin cancers or people who have moles should not use any composition with phototoxic materials included, especially if these people spend a lot of time in the sun. The most common phototoxic materials in use are *cold-pressed* citrus oils, but also include angelica root and verbena absolute.

Sensitization – Sensitization usually occurs after exposure to an undiluted raw material. Sensitization is an immune response to the materials with which the body comes in contact; the result is usually inflammation and pain at the area where the fragrance was applied, or a full-body reaction with skin rash or irritation. Sensitization can also manifest as an asthma attack, rash, runny nose and other respiratory reactions, and neurological symptoms such as headache and foggy thinking.

Carcinogen – Carcinogenic means the raw material has been shown through scientific study to cause cancer.

Neurotoxic – A Neurotoxin is a poison which causes damage to neural/nerve tissues. Plant neurotoxins include, but are not limited to clove, pennyroyal, nutmeg and hyssop (see restricted/prohibited list).

Cross-sensitization occurs when a person who is sensitized to a particular constituent or chemical within an essential oil or raw material is exposed to a different essential oil or raw material which has the same chemical constituent. For example, if a client is sensitized to cloves essential oil, which contains methyl eugenol, it is possible that they will be sensitized to any other essential oils which contain methyl eugenol, such as cassia or rose oils.

Irritation – Irritation is a temporary reaction to an irritant (see list of restricted/prohibited materials), usually manifesting as redness, itching or burning. Once the irritant is removed, the irritation subsides. Irritation usually occurs with people who have sensitive skin, or when an undiluted raw material is used on the skin. Remove the irritant by washing with soap and water.

Restricted Materials

Angelica root *angelica archangelica* (phototoxic) – restricted – up to 4.0000% in a perfume compound

Bergamot cold-pressed *citrus bergamia* (phototoxic) – restricted – less than 4.0000% in a perfume compound (contains restricted chemicals *citral, geraniol, and bergaptene, a psoralen/furanocoumarin, which causes phototoxicity*)** Bergaptene free bergamot usage at less than 30.0000% in a perfume compound (contains restricted chemical *citral*)

Bitter orange cold-pressed *citrus aurantium* (phototoxic) – restricted – less than 10.0000% in a perfume compound (contains restricted chemical *citral, citronellol*)**

Cassia *cinnamomum cassia* (sensitizer/irritant) – restricted – less than 1.0000% in a perfume compound (contains restricted chemicals *benzyl benzoate, cinnamyl alcohol, cinnamaldehyde, eugenol, methyl eugenol*)

Cinnamon bark *cinnamomum zeylanicum* (sensitizer/irritant) – restricted – less than 8.0000% in a perfume compound (contains restricted chemicals *cinnamaldehyde, cinnamyl alcohol, eugenol*)

Clove *syzygium aromaticum* (sensitizer/irritant) – restricted – less than 6.0000% in a perfume compound(contains restricted chemicals *benzyl alcohol, eugenol, isoeugenol, farnesol, methyl eugenol*)

Cumin *cuminum cyminum* (phototoxic) – restricted – less than 5.0000% in a perfume compound

Grapefruit cold-pressed *citrus paradisi* (phototoxic) – restricted – less than 8.0000% in a perfume compound (contains restricted chemicals *citral, citronellol, farnesol, geraniol*)**

Lemon cold-pressed *citrus limonum* (phototoxic) – restricted – less than 10.0000% in a perfume compound (contains restricted chemicals *citral, citronellol, geraniol*)**

Lime cold-pressed *citrus aurantifolia* (phototoxic) – restricted – less than 15.0000% in a perfume compound (contains restricted chemical *citral*)**

Tagettes/Tagetes *tagetes patula, T. minuta, T. erecta* (phototoxic) – restricted – less than 0.1000% in a perfume composition – *T. minuta* CO2 extract usage levels less than 0.1000% in perfume compound – *T. patula* usage levels less than 1.0000% in finished perfume compound – *T. erecta* usage levels less than 2.0000% in finished perfume compound (each contains at least one of restricted chemical(s) *eugenol, 2-hexen-1-al, geraniol, citronellol*)

Oakmoss *evernia prunastri spp.* (sensitizer) – restricted – less than 0.1000% in perfume compound ~ Category 11 includes all non-skin contact or incidental skin contact products. Due to the negligible skin contact from these types of products there is no justification for a restriction of the concentration of this fragrance ingredient in the finished product (per The Good Scents Company website, used with permission) ~ According to a paper submitted by the Scientific Committee on Consumer Product (SCCP) published at ec.europa.eu, atranol and chloratranol are the main chemical components in *evernia prunastri* (per IFRA) responsible for sensitization. The IFRA recommends use of evernia prunastri which has had these sensitizing chemicals removed. IFRA's 43rd Amendment seeks to ban oak moss (as well as ylang-ylang and jasmine) due to its sensitizing characteristics

Peru balsam *myroxylon pereirae* extracts and distillates (sensitizer) – restricted – extracts and distillates of Peru balsam (the exudation from Myroxylon pereirae (Royle) Klotzsch) should not be used such that the total level exceeds 0.4% in cosmetic products. Based on a wide variety of test results on the sensitizing potential of Peru balsam and its derivatives

(The Good Scents Company website, used with permission)

Pine *pinaceae mugo, P. sylvatica, P. nigra, P. pinaster (sensitizer)* – restricted -- pertains to peroxides formed within the distillates with ageing – *pinaceae mugo* usage levels less than 8.0000% in perfume compound; *p. sylvatica* usage levels: no information found; *p. nigra* usage levels less than 5.0000% in perfume compound; *p. pinaster* usage levels: no information found

Rue *ruta graveolens* (phototoxic) – restricted – less than 2.0000% in perfume
Compound

Verbena ABSOLUTE *lippia citriodora* (sensitizer) – absolute restricted – "should not be used as a fragrance ingredient at a level over 1% in fragrance compounds" per the IFRA

Tea absolutes *Camellia sinensis, thea chinensis, thea sinensis* (sensitizer) – restricted – no current usage level percentage suggested

Treemosses *usnea / pseudoevernia furfuracea* (sensitizer) — see restrictions relating to oak moss

Wintergreen (toxic) – redistilled Chinese variety (gaultheria procumbens l. leaf oil) can be used up to 3.0000% in fragrance

Wormwood *artemesia absinthium* (sensitizer) – see extensive information at www.thegoodscentscompany.com regarding artemesia absinthium l. Cuba, Artemisia absinthium l. oil Italy, Artemisia absinthium l. oil Poland; can be used up to 2.0000% in fragrance compound

Prohibited Materials

Almond, bitter unrectified *prunus amygdalus v. amara (toxic)* – less than 3.0000% in perfume compound (can use the 40/60 blend of bitter almond and sweet almond oils approved by the US DEA), or almond oil free from prussic acid (FFPA) *(prussic acid = hydrocyanic acid = cyanide)*

Birch, sweet CRUDE *betula lenta* (toxic) – *rectified only – see the IFRA website for complete information,* can be used up to 0.5000 % in fragrance compounds

Cade unrectified *juniperus oxycedrus* (carcinogenic/irritant/genotoxicity) — *limited use – see the IFRA website for complete information –* cade oil rectified can be used up *to* 0.5000% in a perfume compound (total PHA's)

Calamus *acorus calamus* (carcinogenic) – banned as a food and medicinal additive in 1968 by the FDA – no studies found regarding calamus leaf oil; TGSC indicates usage up to 3.0000% in a perfume compound – rhizome recommended at less than 4.0000% in a perfume compound – (contains *methyl eugenol*), cis- and trans-Asarone as such should not be used as fragrance ingredients; essential oils containing cis- or trans-asarone (e.g. calamus oils) should not be used at a level such that the total concentration of cis- and trans-asarone exceeds 0.01% in consumer products

Costus root *saussurea lappa* (sensitizer) – concrete and absolute PROHIBITED for use in perfumery/fragrance

Fig leaf *ficus carica* (sensitizer) – PROHIBITED; no additional information found

Massoia bark *cryptocaryo massoio* – PROHIBITED, should not be used in fragrance or flavor

Melissa *melissa officinalis* – PROHIBITED (contains high levels of *citral* and *geraniol*)

Peru balsam *crude resin* *myroxylon pereirae* (sensitizer) – PROHIBITED – s*ee Peru balsam extracts and distillates in the restricted list*

above

Savin *juniperus sabina* L. (sensitizer) – PROHIBITED

Sassafras *sassafras albidum, sassafras officinale* (carcinogenic/toxic) – PROHIBITED – not for use in fragrance – 75% safrole; safrole is prohibited and is not to exceed 0.01% of *total* safrole in a perfume compound

Styrax gum resin aka benzoin (sensitizer) – PROHIBITED – crude gum is prohibited; extracts and distillates of styrax gum resin/benzoin are restricted

Tansy *tanacetum vulgare* variety (toxic) – PROHIBITED

Verbena OIL *lippia citriodora* (sensitizer) – PROHIBITED and should not be used as a perfume/fragrance ingredient (contains restricted chemicals *citral, citronellol, geraniol*)

This may not be a complete list of restricted and prohibited materials, and it is not presented as such. It is important to fully research each raw material intended for use in perfume composition.

Restricted/Prohibited *Chemicals* within Natural Raw Materials

Chemicals in many raw materials which are restricted or prohibited by the IFRA include, but are not limited to:

Methyl eugenol
Eugenol
Cinnamaldehyde
Cinnamyl alcohol
Citronellol
Citral

Isoeugenol
Farnesol
Geraniol
Safrole
Psoralens
Polynuclear aromatic hydrocarbons (PAH)
Furanocoumarin/Furocoumarin containing oils:

> (angelica root oil, bergamot oil cold-pressed, bitter orange oil cold-pressed, cumin oil, grapefruit oil cold-pressed, lemon oil cold pressed, lime oil cold-pressed, rue oil)

The IFRA has recently restricted the usage of jasmine, both the grandiflorum and sambac varieties, based on the inclusion of some small amounts of restricted chemicals in their composition. Jasmine grandiflorum contains the restricted chemicals benzyl benzoate, eugenol, (E)-isoeugenol, (Z)-isoeugenol and farnesol; jasmine sambac contains the restricted chemicals benzyl alcohol, benzyl benzoate, eugenol, farnesol, geraniol and (E)-2-hexen-1-al. Both contain far more chemicals than those which are restricted, including skatoles and indoles, which give jasmine oils their distinctive heady narcotic, almost poopy smell, which we humans find irresistible.

"Quenching"

Quenching is purportedly a phenomenon in which it is believed some sensitizing chemicals can be rendered safe (quenched) for skin contact by adding a quenching agent. According to Textbook of Contact Dermatitis by Richard J.G. Rycroft, Torkil Menne, Peter J. Frosch and Claude Benezra, "Another interesting phenomenon regarding perfume allergy is the quenching phenomenon described by Opdyke [10]. He observed that the three aldehydes, i.e. cinnamic aldehyde, phenylacetaldehyde, and citral, proved to be skin sensitizers but that the essential oil in which the aldehyde naturally occurs did not induce sensitization, even though the aldehyde was present in concentrations as high as 85%. It appeared that some other component(s) of the natural oil might inhibit the induction or expression of sensitization. This was called the "quenching" phenomenon. However, details were lacking and his results could not be reproduced; Basketter [11], who performed extensive studies in the guinea pig using the two "quenching" pairs, cinnamic aldehyde and eugenol, and citral and limonene, failed to provide any support for this phenomenon."

The IFRA no longer supports the phenomenon of quenching as a means of suppressing skin-sensitizing chemicals within a fragrance/perfume compound. The EU Cosmetic Directive has adopted the IFRA's standing on quenching.

While we as natural perfumers might not agree with some of the low or no usage levels of the raw materials which are listed as 'restricted' and 'prohibited' by the IFRA and adopted by the EU Cosmetic Directive, it is important to have the safety information available, as well as a means of researching raw materials, so that we can make informed decisions when formulating a perfume composition.

Endangered Species & Cruelty in Perfumery

Ambergris, the exudate from sperm whales, was once a very important part of perfume history. Ambergris is believed to be a result of stomach irritation caused by undigested bits of cuttlefish beaks which the whale vomits into the sea. When fresh, ambergris has an off-putting fecal odor, but when aged upon the world's oceans for decades, it takes on a pleasant, heavy seaweed-like scent that proved very useful in creating perfumes. Today trade in ambergris is illegal in most countries. Trading continues with approximately 4% of ambergris used for perfumery being beach combed, the rest being harvested as a result of Japanese and Norwegian whale hunting. *"Included in Appendix I of the Convention on International Trade in Endangered Species of Wild Flora and Fauna (CITES) since 1985, making trade in products (i.e. sperm oil, teeth, and ambergris) illegal in most countries. Since 1981, importation of sperm oil and other sperm whale products has been banned by the European Union. Importation of marine mammal products in the U.S. has been banned since 1972 (Whitehead 2003). "*

The civet, commonly referred to as civet cat, is not a cat at all.

Civets are part of the Viverridae family, which includes genets, Binturong or "bearcats", and linsangs, and more closely resemble ferrets or mongoose in appearance than cats. Civet paste was a staple of antiquarian perfumery, used to fix, extend and exalt the scent a perfume. The paste is obtained by first agitating the civet, usually by poking sticks through the holes in the cage in which it's trapped. The 'agitation process' causes the civet to excrete the desired substance from glands near its anus, then the civet is captured and the exudate is scraped from the glands. Though the commercial harvesting of civet paste has diminished considerably in modern perfumery in the past few decades, use of civet paste in NBP is prevalent. Chanel reports they have replaced the civet used in *Chanel No.5* with a synthetic approximation, and have been doing so since 1998. Currently there is a market for another civet product, Kopi Luwak, a specialty coffee. Kopi Luwak is the end product (no pun intended) of the Asian Palm Civets' consuming and digesting (whole) native coffee beans. The beans are then picked from the dung, roasted, and sold for a small fortune, a much more humane way of utilizing the talented back end of a civet. The scent of civet paste is nauseatingly fecal, heavy and musky, but tinctured to 1-3%, it has a little of those offensive notes, and offers expansiveness to perfume compositions when used in very small doses.

Musk deer, native to Asia, have been protected by the International CITES since 1979, however, trade in musk deer pods has increased. It is estimated there are fewer than 3000 (down from an estimated 30,000 in 1986) musk deer in India today as poaching has greatly diminished their numbers. The male musk deer has a sac or pod in which the musk is produced, and the animal is often killed to retrieve the pods. There are tiny grains within the musk pod that when properly dried, tinctured and used sparingly adds a roundness and harmonious "completeness" to a perfume. Musk was an important aromatic in ancient perfumery as it provided deliciously attractive animalic warmth which was highly favored. Natural Botanical Perfumers can and do use botanically derived "musks" from ambrette seed and through artful formulation of other natural and botanical elements.

Castoreum is obtained from sacs located near the anus of the European and North American beaver. It is produced by both the male and female beaver, and is mixed with the urine of the animal and spread around as a means of marking territory. In perfumery, castoreum sacs are cut from the animal's body and allowed to dry for several years, often smoked to cure, then tinctured in alcohol. It lends a leathery, tobacco-like, musky, animalic note to chypre, fougere and Oriental style perfumes.

With a few exceptions, most of these essences can be approximated botanically through the artful and practiced combination of animalic notes such as ambrette, choya loban, nagarmotha, cepes, patchouli and others.

Another important consideration of the natural perfumer is how long to keep the materials in the perfumer's palette. Some studies have shown that citrus oils are the most volatile of oils in this regard, requiring disposal and replacement within one year of purchase. According to Ingrid Martin in her book *Aromatherapy for Massage Practitioners,* citrus oils can be kept safely for up to 18 months, so long as they are kept at a continuous temperature away from direct sunlight, and in a dry environment. Old citrus oils oxidize and other oils with high levels of linalool form peroxides which are much more dermal sensitizing than fresher oils.

Sue Clarke, author of *Essential Chemistry for Safe Aromatherapy,* states that "the rate of deterioration [of essential oils] doubles for every 10°C rise in temperature".

It is known that storing raw materials in colored glass, away from direct light, and away from extreme heat and moisture does contribute to their longevity. To prevent oxidation of oils in large or half-empty bottles, either transfer the unused portion of raw material into a smaller bottle, or utilize small glass marbles or glass beads (drop them in one at a time) to maintain the level of material in the bottle as close to the opening of the bottle as is possible. Another way in which to preserve the integrity of the raw materials is through the use of an oxygen barrier, a combination of inert gases primarily made up of nitrogen and argon. This gas is heavier than air and sinks to the top of the liquid preventing the oxygen in the air from contacting the essential oil (raw material) thus preventing oxidization. This same system can be used to preserve the longevity of carrier oils. This inert gas can be purchased at Nature's Gift from their website at www.naturesgift.com or at Wine Preserve at their website at www.winepreserve.com, or at a local wine store.

Some raw materials, such as patchouli, sandalwood and vetyver, are more desirable when aged, though if poorly stored, they too can take on a strange off note or change chemically. Well-aged, poorly stored sandalwood, for example, takes on a resinous almost pickle-like scent. One thing to note is that if oil takes on a rancid cooking oil scent, it is likely that it has been adulterated as a common adulterant is clear vegetable oil. With sandalwood in particular, this is very common. Having been enlightened, dear student, to the terms of measurement utilized to determine an essences life expectancy, it is important to remember that the procurement of *vintage* and *antique* oils is of utmost importance to a Natural Botanical Perfumer. A fabulously famous Natural Botanical Perfumer and Aromatherapist indicated during a conversation, after having shared an oil which was at least a half century past its prime, that though an oil may not be useable in a formulation, it is still useful as an historical reference.

Always store your raw materials in glass or aluminum containers, never in plastic, as the raw materials are solvents and can deteriorate plastics, creating holes and leaks in the container. When purchasing larger volumes of raw materials (kilos), the supplier (if he/she is reputable and knowledgeable) will usually ship the order in aluminum, rarely in glass, and (should) never in plastic. There are some suppliers, however, who will ship in plastic containers to save shipping costs, but they normally inform the customer of this prior to shipping so an appropriate storage container can be acquired prior to the oil's arrival in which to transfer the raw material when it arrives. When using dropper style caps on dilutions or whole, undiluted materials, it is important not to draw the liquid all the way into the rubber bulb of the cap. Over time, the raw material will degrade and deteriorate the rubber bulb causing leaks and contamination of the raw material inside the bottle.

Because of the number and variety of natural botanical essences, it is important to study and learn the Latin nomenclature of the essences used in your formulations. For example, instead of using just the word *rose* in a formulation, write the Latin *rosa damascena* or the name of whatever rose is being used. This is simply for personal identification purposes as, unfortunately, many essential oils and other aromatics used in perfumery are not marketed or sold under their true Latin names, and even more unfortunately, some growers don't even know what the Latin names are! One of the most confusing aspects of using Latin nomenclature when ordering essences is that some names are in dispute, or the essence has the unlucky fortune of possessing more than one – for example, opoponax, or sweet myrrh, is named *O. chromium* by Julia Lawless in her book *The Illustrated Encyclopedia of Essential Oils,* and *Commiphora erythrea varietas glabrescent* by Steffan Arctander in his seminal work, *Perfume and Flavor Materials of Natural Origin.*

For the sake of identification, use both the Latin and the common names provided by the supplier.

There are several websites dedicated to providing the apprentice perfumer with research information pertaining to the chemical constituents of many natural botanical fragrances. Dr. Duke's Phytochemical & Ethnobotanical Databases at www.ars-grin.gov/duke/ and The Good Scents Company at www.thegoodscentscompany.com have comprehensive databases which many Natural Botanical Perfumers utilize to research chemical compounds found within specific natural oils. Bo Jensen, at www.bojensen.net, has created a guide to natural fragrance and flavors which is also useful. Local universities often allow public access to their library, it would be wise to check out a few of the more in-depth essential oil chemistry books available, such as E. Joy Bowles' *The Chemistry of Aromatherapeutic Oils* or Robert Tisserand's *Essential Oil Safety, A Guide for Health Care Practioners.* The local public library may also have copies of these guides on their shelves.

The most sought after guide or research tool for the Natural Botanical Perfumer who wishes to study fragrance chemicals is Steffen Arctander's *Perfume and Flavor Materials of Natural Origin* published by Allured Publishing. In it are listed over 500 natural fragrances.

Essential oils, absolutes, concretes and other Natural Botanical Perfumery raw materials each contain hundreds, if not thousands, of chemical constituents.

The primary chemical constituents in essential oils, absolutes and other Natural Botanical Perfumery materials are terpenes, which are comprised of monoterpenes and sesquiterpenes; and alcohols, esters, phenols, coumarins, ketones and lactones. These chemicals are broken down into two standard groups: Hydrocarbons and Oxygenated Compounds.

Hydrocarbons

Monoterpenes
Monoterpenes are found in many essential oils but are prevalent in citrus oils. Their qualities are tonic and antiseptic and they also act as air purifiers. Monoterpenes are made up of ten carbon atoms. Colorless and highly volatile, they deteriorate rapidly and must be kept at cooler temperatures. Examples of monoterpenes are limonene found in most citrus oils, pinene found in pine, and camphene found in camphor.

Sesquiterpenes
Less volatile than monoterpenes, sesquiterpenes are made up of fifteen carbon atoms. Sesquiterpenes have a calming effect. They are ant-inflammatory and anti-infectious. Examples of sesquiterpenes are zingiberene found in ginger, cedrene found in cedarwood, and caryophellene found in clove.

Oxygenated Compounds

Phenols
Phenols are the most antiseptic of all the chemical constituents found in plants. They can be stimulating and beneficial in very small doses, but in larger doses they can be nervous system toxins. Larger doses of phenols may also cause skin irritation and digestive sensitivities. Examples of phenols are thymol found in thyme, and eugenol found in clove.

Alcohols
Alcohols are antibacterial, antibiotic, anti-fungal and antiseptic and are a good tonic for the nervous system. They can also stimulate immune response. Examples of alcohols are lavendulol found in lavender, nerol found in neroli and geraniol found in geranium.

Esters & Ethers

Ethers are somewhat stronger than esters, but both have very similar properties. They are both powerful anti-inflammatories, antispasmodics, and both are antibacterial. They are gentle on the skin and efficient in relaxing and rebalancing the nervous system. Examples of ethers and esters include cinnamyl acetate found in cinnamon, and myrtinyl acetate found in myrtle.

Ketones

Ketones can be relaxing and sedating in small doses. They also can help with the healing of scar tissues and are known anticoagulants. They are also useful in stimulating the immune system and treating respiratory ailments. In larger doses, they have the opposite effect and can be toxic to the nervous system. Examples of ketones are thyone found in sage, pinocamphone found in hyssop and carvone found in peppermint.

Aldehydes

Aldehydes have properties which are similar to alcohols and ketones. They can be calming to the nervous system and are anti-inflammatory. Aldehydes can be somewhat caustic and cause irritation to skin and mucous membranes. Examples of aldehydes include furfurol found in lavender, sandalwood, cinnamon and cypress, and aldehyde benzoic found in benzoin.

Coumarins/Lactones

Coumarins can be relaxing and sedating. They have properties which are known to be anticonvulsant and anti-coagulating. Furocoumarins (or furanocoumarins) are of major concern due to their photosensitivity. Examples of coumarins include bergaptene found in bergamot, angelicine found in angelica, and citroptene found in most citrus

CHAPTER 4

Gather Ye Rosebuds While Ye May …

The internet can be a great source of information for the study of NBP. It can also be a great source of frustration. With all the misleading information on the 'net, it is wise to conduct extensive research and jump down a few "rabbit holes" to find what is being sought. Studying scientific papers on the internet is important, culling information from such places as Science Direct, Nature-International Weekly Journal of Science, and the Ngai Lab at UC Berkeley. Most of these are for-profit and will charge a small fee to download and print scientific studies done on perfumery and olfaction, but the education is worth every penny spent.

Other sources include the *short-cut-to-everything-IFRA* at The Good Scents Company, and the IFRA online. The IFRA's online site has a lot of useful information, though their website can be difficult to maneuver due to the manner in which they classify and identify aromatics. Another way to source information is to cull the bibliographies of both scientific papers found online, and perfume-related books. In a snowball effect, one book can reveal the way to more books, and those books to even more books. For example, an obscure reference on an online aromatherapy web page pertaining to "Carmelite Water" might lead to another obscure website featuring PDF files of *Mackenzies 5000 Receipts,* and further exploration might lead to an almost-impossible-to-find PDF publication of the *Encyclopedia of Practical Receipts and Processes* by William B. Dick, wherein may be found not only a near-original recipe for Carmelite Water, or *Eau de Carmes,* but what may be discovered are techniques for distillation, or alcohometry and specific gravity, information necessary for standardizing tinctures and evulsions.

As an example of what can be discovered in bibliographies, in the book *The Nose, A Profile of Sex, Beauty, and Survival,* Gabrielle Glaser, the author, has researched and referenced such works as *the Bible*, *Scents of Time* by Edmund Morris, *Scent: The Mysterious and Essential Powers of Smell*, by Annick LeGuerer, and works found online: *The Florentine Chronicle* by Marchione di Coppo Stefani, written in the 14th century, with a translation into English found at http://www2.iath.virginia.edu/osheim/marchione.html.

Reference and cross-reference as much of the information as possible as this may be the best source for furthering an academic perfume education. Keep in mind that not all the information retrieved will be accurate. Again, jump down a few rabbit holes to get to the original source.

Vintage & Antique Oil Collecting

Acquiring vintage and antique raw materials for perfumery is often just a one-click bid away. Many Natural Botanical Perfumers spend a great deal of time and money obtaining rare vintage and antique raw materials through sources such as Ebay, through private collections, at flea markets, auctions and estate sales, and less often at garage and yard sales. A great deal of vintage and antique bottles sold on Ebay is acquired by the seller through auctions of lots of materials from old turn-of-the-century pharmacies and drugs stores. Some of these original buys are quite old, dating as far back as 40 or 50 years ago, with the current owners just recently letting go of a bottle here and there, or as less often happens, entire lots of dozens of bottles.

The demand for vintage oil collecting has increased as the number of Natural Botanical Perfumers has increased. Horror stories pop up on occasion about unethical collectors and sellers making surreptitious deals, bargaining off individual bottles from auction lots without the current bidders of the items being aware. Only when the parcel arrives does the bidder realize that they have been ripped off. In these cases there is often little recourse.

There are also stories of happy fortune as well. One perfumer/collector recounted her experience of purchasing a lot of antique oils for which she paid a very reasonable price. Excited about the prospect of receiving the oils, her joy was magnified when she discovered a nearly full one ounce bottle of vintage Mysore sandalwood tucked in the parcel, which the seller gifted her, clearly unaware of its value.

When conducting an online search for vintage and antique oils, or while digging through boxes at a flea market or antiques' fair, a few of the more popular perfume ingredient manufacturers' names to look for are:

Fritzsche Brothers
Dodge & Olcott
Magnus, Maybee & Reynard
Givaudan

Less popular are:

Field & Company (Aromatics)
Archer-Daniels Midland Co., Ltd.
Plaimar Limited
Schimmel
W.J. Bush & Co., Ltd.
Antoine Chiris Ltd.
Mallagh & Co.
C.W. Field Ltd.
Payan & Bertrand
Robertet
Albert & Laloue Camilli
Charabot & Co.
C.A. Charpentier
Bruno Court
Pierre Dhumez
Flora Aromatics Co., Ltd.
W.H. Hobbs & Co., Ltd.
Lautier Fils, Ltd.
Victor Mane Fils
Old Strand Chemical & Drug Co.
A.W. Munns Co.
Natural & Synthetic Perfumery Essence Company

Stanley Nicholas & Co.
Roure Bertrand Fils
P. Samuelson & Co.
Schmoller & Bompard
Tombarel Freres
Alfred Paul White
Wilson & Mansfield, Ltd.

Gather Ye Tools. The following bottles are recommended ~ twenty to sixty 5 ml or 10 ml bottles for dilutions; five 1 oz blue cobalt or amber bottles with caps for storing accords or finished perfumes compounds; five 2 oz blue cobalt or amber bottles with caps, also for storing accords or finished perfume compounds; two 4 oz blue cobalt bottles with caps for storing larger batches of accords or finished perfume compounds, and an assortment of 8 and 16 oz to one liter or comparable sized bottles for formulating and maturing finished perfume compositions. Expand upon these bottle sizes and capacities, including bottles in which to present the finished perfumes. Also needed are ten to fifteen glass droppers with rubber bulbs. Be sure to purchase the same size droppers as this is important when formulating perfume trials. The droppers will be used to measure alcohol and raw materials to create the dilutions, and for measuring dilutions into a perfume composition, or choose to use disposable plastic pipettes. Small plastic or metal funnels, approximately 1 to 2 inches across are also required, and they are used to pour perfumes from the formulation bottle into the final perfume bottle, and for fining, or clarifying, a perfume composition. Coffee filter papers are sufficient for filtering out larger pieces of perfume dregs (the little bits and pieces of solid perfume material floating about in a composition), but usually won't create a crystal clear perfume without more fining/clarifying techniques being applied, or by use of laboratory filter papers. While a composition will run freely (usually) through a coffee filter paper, it will not so easily through a laboratory filter paper. Laboratory filter paper is designed to catch minute bits of perfume dreg that a coffee filter is not designed to catch.

Other materials required for a beginner are isopropyl alcohol for cleaning droppers and bottles; self-adhesive labels or waterproof self-adhesive labels for labeling dilution bottles, composition bottles, etc.; scent strips for evaluating dilutions and trials and finished perfume compositions. Purchase scent strips or a watercolor sketch book of acid-free watercolor paper, and cut the paper into squares or into strips and use them for evaluations. Small glass or metal cups, those used for culinary condiments, are useful for rinsing used droppers in isopropyl alcohol.

Pour out used alcohol, either the diluent or the iso-cleaner, after using it. Some perfumers pour the used up alcohols into a open bowl or cup and allow them to evaporate naturally so as not to further pollute their water systems by flushing it or pouring it down the drain. Purchase pipe cleaners and a small bottle brush, such as those used for baby bottles, for cleaning the inside of droppers and bottles after use. A good brand of bottle brushes is Dr. Brown's Natural Flow cleaning brushes as they are BPA, PVC, lead and phthalates-free. The diluent of choice for this manual is organic grain or grape alcohol, and nearly all study is focused on its use as the base of a perfume compositions. As some using this manual may discover, organic grain/grape alcohol is not always easy to come by, and it is almost prohibitively expensive, a gallon costing somewhere in the neighborhood of $200 USD, not including hazardous materials fees and shipping costs.

So as a substitute it is acceptable to use a naturally denatured ethanol/alcohol, which is sold in smaller volumes and is a bit less expensive than its organic natural counterpart, or organic liquid oil, either jojoba or fractionated coconut can be used. It is important that meticulous notes are kept on every dilution, blending idea, trial, composition trial, finished perfume, et al, in order to replicate the perfumes created.

Avoid using cork top bottles for dilutions or to store compositions as over time the contents of the bottle will evaporate. Corks do not provide a sufficient enough seal unless sealed with wax appropriate to the job, and they tend to break easily in the neck of the bottle. Cork top bottles are nice for the sake of aesthetics and display, but shouldn't be used for any alcohol-based perfume or perfumery materials long-term.

It is also not a good idea to store finished compositions in rubber sealed bottles as over time the diluent eats away and erodes the rubber, causing a leak in the seal and ultimately the untimely evaporation of the perfume. Reduce, reuse, recycle ~ using old wine bottles with screw top lids, old olive oil bottles, or any other recycled bottle, preferably made with colored glass, and as long as they've been thoroughly cleaned, are perfect for long-term storage of finished compositions and finished evulsions and tinctures, and using these recycled materials spares the additional expense of buying boxes of new glass bottles.

Shallow plastic bins with lids can be used to store bottles of raw materials, diluted materials and tools. Be sure to keep everything separate; a plastic bin specifically for each type of tool, i.e. all raw undiluted materials in one bin; all diluted materials in another bin; clean empty bottles, funnels and other clean tools in another bin. This keeps everything properly organized and prevents contamination of clean equipment. For example, if scent strips, water color strips, coffee filters or laboratory filters are stored in a bin with any raw material, diluted or not, the strips and filters would eventually absorb the scent of those aromatics, rendering them useless for perfumery formulation.

There several steps to properly cleaning perfumer's tools. Begin with a bucket of hot soapy water, wash and rinse the tools, then move them to a pot of warm water in which baking soda has been added to help deodorize and further clean the tools. Some tools, such as dropper bulbs, will require more cleaning than glass or metal as the scent of the raw materials used in perfume formulation may "stick" and permeate the rubber. Once the tools have been washed or soaked, rinse them thoroughly and allow them to air dry. It is not recommended that they go into a dishwasher as there is a possibility that they will not become clean enough for future formulation.

Just before using the tools in formulating sessions, rinse or wipe them down with alcohol, isopropyl 70% or organic grape or grain alcohol. Sterilizing glass and metal tools in boiling water just prior to use is also recommended.

This cleaning ritual is especially important if there are indoor pets in the perfumer's studio. Use bins with tight-fitting lids, and keep everything off of the ground. Also throw away any tools which cannot be cleaned of scent, they are no longer useful for formulation.

The raw materials available to today's Natural Botanical Perfumer are far more numerous than they were for our predecessors. Where their palettes were restricted to a few dozen or so essences, ours has been greatly expanded to include hundreds of materials.

Raw Materials

Absolute ~ usually alcohol extracted and obtained directly from concretes

Butaflor ~ butane extraction of hard to distill aromatics which are not offered in the open market, such as mountain misery (*Chamaebatia foliolosa);* simple home extraction method utilizing a 'honey extractor' and canned butane (attempt at your own risk); can also be used to extract absolutes from homemade pomades

CO2 extraction ~ carbon dioxide extractions, supercritical carbon dioxide extracts. Solvent extraction utilizing CO2 at low temperature and high pressure to create a fragrant product

Co-distillation ~ steam or hydro distillation of a fragrant material into another fragrant material (usually sandalwood). Mitti attar is a co-distillation of baked earth into sandalwood oil

Concrete ~ obtained through solvent extraction of a botanical material resulting in a waxy substance that is highly fragrant; butane home solvent extraction is now an option for NBP's

Destructive distillation ~ distillation of materials, seashells or resins, which are intentionally burned, resulting in a material with a smoky, leathery bouquet

Enfleurage ~ ancient method of obtaining scent by repeatedly placing, removing and replacing fragrant botanical   materials on sheets of glass that have been glazed with fat (typically cleaned animal fat)

Essential Oil ~ steam distilled, hydro distilled or cold pressed from botanical material

Evulsion ~ a method of extraction in which the use of an ultrasonic device (jewelry cleaner) is utilized via sonication to produce high grade perfumery materials by placing the plant material into a container filled with a solvent (natural perfumers use alcohol) and placing the container into a water bath inside the ultrasonic device,   allowing the sonic waves to extract the scent molecules from the plant material

Floral water/hydrosol/hydrolat ~ fragrant watery portion of distillation used in place of distilled water in a perfume compound, or as a toner and tonic for skin care

Floral wax ~ waxy material left behind after an absolute has been extracted from concrete. This material can be important to the production of solid perfumes

Pomade ~ fatty substance obtained by enfleurage; the pomade is then used for solid perfume making, or it is further processed by soaking the pomade in high proof alcohol for several weeks to obtain a fragrant tincture which is filtered and used to make alcohol based perfume

Tincture ~ extraction of essence from botanical or animal materials which are left to soak in a 190 proof alcohol   bath oftentimes resulting in a fragrant material which rivals the strength of an absolute; no heat or sonication is applied

Perfume Menstruum or Medium

The alcohol used must be of the highest proof and grade available. The use of vodka or other 'drinking' alcohol for use in perfumes for sale is prohibited by law in all US states, regardless of whether taxes are paid. Drinking alcohol does not make an adequate menstruum for perfume making as the alcohol content is too low, the higher grades being around 40%. Organic grain and grape alcohols (rectified spirits) are at 95% alcohol content. Check with the local government, state or country's regulations pertaining the use and sale of perfumery appropriate undenatured alcohols. Perfumers' denatured alcohol may be used, but if the manufacturer denatures with a synthetic denaturant, it may not be acceptable to call these perfumes 'natural'. There are naturally denatured perfumer's alcohols on the market, however, in order to pass regulation so large an amount of the natural denaturant is necessary to pass regulation that it often lends itself as a scenting agent and can ruin a perfume formulation. A denaturant is used to prevent abuse of these higher grades of alcohol, rendering them useless for drinking.

Oil-based perfumes can be made in high grade jojoba (preferably organic), or in fractionated coconut oil. Both of these oils have long shelf lives and do not go rancid.

Solid perfumes are typically made in a base of beeswax with added base oils (jojoba or fractionated coconut). Floral waxes are also used in solid perfume.

CHAPTER 5

Working the Bench . . .

In the movie *Perfume: Story of a Murderer,* Baldini the Perfumer goes into some detail about the construction of a perfume, showing Grenouille how perfume is built with notes and accords, the only problem is that Baldini is discussing a method of perfume construction which isn't invented for nearly 100 years from the time frame in which the story is told. Septimus Piesse, 1820-1882, a perfumer and author, created the music-to-perfume scale to classify scent. Mr. Piesse separated each part of the perfume into musically referenced categories ~ top notes, heart notes and base notes; accords and chords.

From the book *The Science and Art of Perfumery* by Edward Sagarin, he writes:

"Another contribution to the field of odor classification was made by the famous perfumer and perfume historian, Septimus Piesse. This unique figure in the history of the science created what he called an "odophone." The odors were like sounds, he pointed out, and a scale could be created going from the first or lowest note, the heavy smell, to the last or highest note, the sharp smell. In between there was an ascending ladder. Each odor note corresponded to a key on his odophone, and in the creation of a happy mixture of many different odors, which we call a "bouquet" and which every finished perfume must be, the creator seeks not only to hit the right notes, but to strike those notes which go with one another. His perfume must not be out of tune.

Septimus Piesse pictured himself in his laboratory coat, a white-haired maestro banging away with inspired harmony at the keys of a fantastic odor piano, his agile fingers bringing forth, not beautiful sounds, but fragrant vapors."

Head/Top notes are typically the first notes smelled in a perfume. They're the opening notes, the lead or hook that draws a person in. This note is relatively fleeting, usually lasting no more than 10 or 20 minutes. Head/Top notes include, but are not limited to:

Anise, basil, bergamot, cardamom, cilantro, Roman chamomile, cinnamon, coriander, davana, grapefruit, lemon, lime, lemongrass, lotus (blue), magnolia, mandarin, tagetes, neroli, petitgrain, bitter and sweet orange, peppermint, clary sage, spearmint, tangerine, verbena, violet leaf.

Heart/Middle notes normally classify or identify the perfume family or *leitmotif* of the composition. For instance, if the perfume family chosen is a white floral, then blend some combination of jasmine, neroli, tuberose, gardenia tinctures and other 'white' flower oils as the main component of this note. Heart notes last much longer than the top notes, and sometimes linger through to the end of the perfume's skin life. Heart/Middle notes include, but are not limited to:

Bay, cananga, caraway, carnation, cassia, carrot seed, chamomile, clary sage, cinnamon, cloves, cypress, fennel, geranium, ginger, ho leaf, ho wood, hyacinth, hyssop, jasmines, jonquil, juniper, lavenders, linden, magnolia, marjoram, mimosa, myrtle, narcissus, neroli, nutmeg, oregano, orris root, osmanthus, palmarosa, peppers, pine needle, roses, rosemary, sages, spikenard, tarragon, thyme, tuberose, yarrow, ylang-ylang.

A few of the head/top and heart/middle categories share a few essences in common. These essences can sometimes be called *bridges* and act in more than one part (head/heart/base) of the composition and can help link each note or accord seamlessly to the next. These bridges can also extend through the entire three accord composition.

Base/Bottom notes are the most tenacious and long-lasting of the three parts, holding down and anchoring the scent to the skin. Base/bottom notes include, but are not limited to:

Aloeswood, balsams, benzoin, beeswax, cedarwoods, choyas, cocoa, frankincense, labdanum, mosses, myrrh, olibanum, opoponax, orris root, oudh, *patchouli, *sandalwood, storax, styrax, tolu, tonka, valerian, vanilla, vetyver.*

The essences listed are by no means complete, but serve only as examples as to how an essence can be classified. Many Natural Botanical Perfumes display the characteristics of crossing notes, for example, a perfume or eau de toilette made with a particularly vibrant frankincense that has characteristics of high, bitter, or resinous notes would "show" those notes early on in the perfume, in the head notes, though the note may have been used in the base or heart of a perfume. Usually, this type of dominating note is present throughout the life of the perfume.

*Mysore Sandalwood, *santalum album*, is endangered and the authentic oil may no longer be available for sale. Other varieties from Asia and Australia are available, *santalum spicatum & santalum austrocaledonicum*, but there is debate as to whether these are ethically harvested and processed (i.e. animal testing, clear cutting forests, and adulteration). Many sandalwood oils on the market today are adulterated with other oils or with synthetics.

Fixatives are raw materials or other natural materials which are used in very small amounts (1 to 3%) to help sustain a perfume, holding it down onto the skin so the scent lasts longer. Some fixatives include:

Distilled water, floral or other plant hydrosols, resin and wood tinctures, styrax benzoin, vegetable glycerin.

Distilled water, floral and plant hydrosols, and one to three percent vegetable glycerin are added after the perfume composition is complete and is combined with the alcohol. Resin and wood tinctures and styrax benzoin are added to the alcohol prior to blending with a perfume composition. Styrax benzoin can be infused into jojoba or fractionated coconut oil to create fixation for oil-based perfumes. It is important that the tinctures and infusions with styrax benzoin are allowed a few weeks to incorporate completely into the diluents as the fixative value increases with ageing. Animal ingredients were once used profusely as a means of fixing and stabilizing a fragrance

Fragrance Families or Fragrance Classifications

Before composing a perfume, another musical reference that refers specifically to the building of a perfume, an idea of how the perfume is to smell should be developed. Find the inspiration for the scent and begin there.

Floral family ~ rose, jasmine, ylang-ylang, cananga, carnation, cassie, lotus, water lily, tuberose, gardenia, violet, rose geranium, hyacinth, jonquil

Hesperides or Citrus family ~ orange, bergamot, lime, lemon, lemongrass, lemon verbena, citron, yuzu, mandarin, grapefruit, petit grain

Oriental family ~ typified by amber (a blend of labdanum/vanilla/styrax-benzoin) and spices

Chypre family ~ typified by key notes of bergamot and oakmoss; woody, mossy with floral citrus top notes

Woody family ~ dominated by *sandalwood, cedar wood, patchouli, vetyver

Green family ~ galbanum, violet leaf, coriander leaf, rose leaf

Leather family ~ nagarmotha, choya loban, choya nakh, tobacco, patchouli, vetyver, costus

Spice family ~ tolu, cassia, cinnamon, clove, nutmeg, cardamom

Fougere family (pronounced *foo-zhayr*) ~ any ferny, mossy scent with lavender at its heart ~ usually includes patchouli, labdanum, vanilla, tonka and benzoin

Amber family ~ ambriene, cistus, labdanum, vanilla, styrax/benzoin, *ambergris

Animalic family ~ ambrette seed, ambergris, hyraceum aka Africa Stone, *civet, *musk deer, choyas

*Endangered; prohibited by law; likely unethically obtained; possible adulteration

These fragrance families can be combined to produce a scent which is green/floral, spicy/amber, citrus/floral, etc.

Perfume Strength

Perfume/Parfum Extrait (extract) – 15 to 40% (sometimes more to the composer's tastes) composition blend to alcohol

Eau de Parfum – 8 to 15% composition blend to alcohol; sometimes incorporates less than 5% distilled water or floral hydrosol

Eau de Toilette – 4 to 8% composition blend to alcohol; incorporates a small percentage of distilled water or floral hydrosol

Eau de Cologne – 3 to 5% composition blend to alcohol; incorporates a small percentage of distilled water or floral hydrosol

Eau Fraiche/Splash or Aftershave – 1 to 3% composition blend to alcohol; incorporates a small percentage of distilled water or floral hydrosol

Oil and solid perfume compositions are usually not classified in the manner above. They are simply referred to as 'oil perfumes' or 'solid perfumes' without a percentage ratio classification, however, they do require more of the basic perfume composition to oil in order to be detected, but the perfume's skin life – the amount of time the scent lasts on the skin – is usually longer than that of alcohol-based perfume. The scent profile of an oil-based perfume can be vastly different from the same formulation in alcohol.

Determining perfume strength using this method can be tedious as one discovers through constant formulation that some essences require higher dilutions to grade than others. For example, the strength of the original composition should determine the so-called grade of the perfume. What may be discovered through diluting a composition is that an eau de toilette behaves as an eau de parfum or extrait based on the strength and tenacity of the original formulation. Many Natural Botanical Perfumers forgo grading their pefumes, calling all their compositions, no matter how dilute, a parfum.

All raw materials must be evaluated by the perfumer prior to their use in a perfume. The perfumer needs to become familiar with the note category or categories, character and safe usage levels of each material. This is, perhaps, the single most important aspect of perfumery that a perfumer must learn. Do not begin to entertain the thought of creating beautiful perfumes without first having fully experienced the materials which go into making them.

For the purpose of completing the lessons in this book, the following raw materials are recommended:

> Bergamot CFC essential oil
> Coriander essential oil
> Geranium essential oil
> Ginger essential oil
> Ho Wood essential oil
> Jasmine sambac absolute
> Cistus/Labdanum essential oil
> Lavender essential oil
> Lemongrass essential oil
> Neroli essential oil
> Patchouli essential oil
> Petit grain essential oil
> Grapefruit (pink) essential oil
> Rose de Mai (rose centifolia) absolute

Vetiver essential oil
Ylang-ylang essential oil
Bulgarian Rose concrete
Oak Moss absolute

Supplemental list of recommended raw materials:

Vanilla (tincture/evulsion/CO2 extract, etc.)
Benzoin
Clary Sage absolute

Diluting for Evaluation and Formulating

Select a handful of materials for evaluation and dilute a small portion of each essence with the medium of choice as follows:

Essential oils ~ dilute between 10% and 50%
Absolutes ~ dilute to 10% or less
Concretes ~ dilute to 10% or less
Tinctures ~ dilute according to strength
Evulsions ~ dilute according to strength
CO2's ~ dilute between 10% and 30%

These are standard dilutions for the purpose of streamlining the learning process within this text. In the trials outlined in this book, the same materials will be used at different dilution levels to better evaluate and understand ratios and strength of scent. For trial evaluations, make dilutions of each raw materials at 1%, 10% and 20%.

As implied previously, these dilution ratios are not written in stone; some essences require dilutions to 1% or less; essences such as angelica, calamus, tolu balsam, cinnamon, choya loban and choya nakh, cassia, Peru balsam and clove, to name a few. Dilutions for some of these materials are based on their potential toxicity and some on strength of scent. Don't be concerned if a raw material doesn't completely break down in the diluents of choice. It is best to allow all the dilutions to sit for a few days before use to ensure the scent has dispersed throughout the diluents – shaking the bottle a few times a day helps with this process.

Some raw materials are sticky or resinous and droppers cannot be used to measure them out. The best way to measure these materials is to weigh them – see "Advanced Perfumers Tools & Techniques".

Drop-by-Drop Dilution Chart

Dilution Ratio	Essence	Alcohol or Oil
1.00%	1 drop	99 drops
5.00%	5 drops	95 drops
10.00%	10 drops	90 drops
20.00%	20 drops	80 drops
30.00%	30 drops	70 drops
40.00%	40 drops	60 drops
50.00%	50 drops	50 drops
60.00%	60 drops	40 drops
70.00%	70 drops	30 drops

Note: Use the same size dropper for blending dilutions.
*Dilute each of the raw materials to this dilution ratio for trial evaluations.

Diluting Raw Materials

Choose the raw material to be diluted and create a label with the name of the raw material and the dilution ratio (1%, 10%, 20%, etc.), plus the name of the supplier, date of purchase, etc. A code system for the raw materials may be a good way to keep the dilutions organized. Simply refer to the code book and write the code number on the label with the dilution ratio, plus the common or Latin name of the raw material and set the label aside until after the dilution is made. Pour about

1/8 cup of isopropyl alcohol into a small glass cup. With a clean dropper, add the raw material by drops, using the Drop-by-Drop Dilution Chart as a guide. Before using the dropper again, rinse the dropper in isopropyl alcohol until clean (wash the dropper with soap and hot water if the raw material is viscous). Be sure the dropper is clean and dry before using it in another material.

Using a clean dropper of the same size used for the raw material, add in the diluents (alcohol/oil). Cap the diluted material and give it a gentle shake. Wipe the bottle to remove any trace of oil or diluent, place the label on the bottle. Set the dilution aside and move on to the next.

Advanced Dilution

An easier and more efficient way to dilute materials is to dilute into larger bottles, two to four ounce bottles. This will provide a larger volume of diluted raw materials to use at any given time, including during the process of formulating a perfume composition to completion. At some point, graduate to even larger dilution amounts, in the range of 8 ounces, 16 ounces and liters.

Coding Materials

Creating a code system for the dilutions is a fairly simple matter. Classify the raw materials into families. For example, the code letter "F" may represent *florals*, while code letter "C" represents *citrus*. The rest of the code is a number. For example, let's imagine a shipment of the following raw materials is received ~ lemongrass, lemon, bergamot, patchouli and jasmine sambac. Classify each of these materials in this manner: "CN1" for lemongrass, which represents the *citronella* family, and "1" indicating it is the first bottle of this class on the code list; "C1" would represent the lemon, "C2" the bergamot, classifying them both in the *citrus* family. Patchouli is sometimes classified in the *woody* family, so patchouli could be coded as "W1". Jasmine sambac is a floral, so that classification would be coded "F1". Once all raw materials have been coded and classified, add them to the code book including the date of purchase, name of supplier, country of origin, extraction method, dilution percentage, and the common and Latin names of the raw material for each of the codes.

Ess. Code	Latin	Common	Supplier	Extr.	Date of Purchase Country of Origin
F = Floral F1	Jasminum sambac	Jasmine sambac	Liberty Natural	solvent	10/08 India
F2	Jasminum grandiflorum	Jasmine grandiflorum	Liberty Natural	solvent	10/08 India
F3	Polianthes tuberosa	Tuberose	Eden Botanicals	solvent	4/08 India
F4	Viola odorata	Violet leaf absolute	Eden Botanicals	solvent	4/08 France
F5	Acacia farnesiana	Cassie	Liberty Natural	solvent	10/08 Egypt
F6	Acacia mearnsii	Mimosa absolute	Liberty Natural	solvent	10/08 India
F7	Iris pallida	Orris butter	Eden Botanical	solvent	4/08 Italy
RF = Rose Floral RF1	Rosa odorata	Tea rose	White Lotus Aromatics	steam distilled	10/08 China
RF2	Rosa damascena	Rose absolute	Eden Botanical	solvent	10/08 Bulgarian
RF3	Rosa centifolia	Rose de Mai absolute	White Lotus Aromatics	solvent	10/08 France
RF4	Rosa damascene	Rose damask	Liberty Natural	solvent	10/08 Morocco
RF5	Cymbopogan martini	Palmarosa	Liberty Natural	steam distilled	10/08 India

Sample Code for Dilution

Essence Code	Latin	Common	Source	Dilution %
RF1	Rosa odorata	Tea rose	WLA	3.00%
RF2	Rosa damascena	Rose absolute	EB	3.00%
RF3	Rosa centifolia	Rose de mai absolute	WLA	3.00%

Sample Bottle Label

RF1	rosa odorata/Tea Rose	WLA	3%

*WLA = White Lotus Aromatics
*EB = Eden Botanical

Prepare separate pages for the master code and whole raw materials and use the information from the master code page to fill in the dilutions code page. Keep the code books in a safe place and make copies if necessary.

Conducting Evaluations

There are many ways to evaluate an essence, but one of the more effective ways, especially with alcohol dilutions, is to drop a few drops onto the skin and allow the alcohol to burn off a bit, about five seconds, before sniffing the essence. If using oil dilutions, allow the essence to warm and diffuse into the air around the skin then begin sniffing the essence. Also use scent strips to evaluate essence, but it must be noted that a completely accurate profile of how a scent will diffuse and evaporate off the skin will not be obtained unless the evaluations are conducted *on* the skin at some point. Keep in mind that each person's skin chemistry is different, and what is perceived from an evaluation on *your* skin may be entirely different on another person's skin. For a complete profile of the essence, it's best to use a combination of skin and strip tests to evaluate. Use only diluted materials for these evaluations, especially on skin evals as they can cause a chemical sensitization using whole raw materials.

  To use scent strips or squares for evaluation, drop a few drops of the diluted essence onto the strip, allow the alcohol to evaporate and then sniff the strip by placing it as close to the nostrils as possible without touching the nose with the strip, and gently sniff it while slightly waving it under the nose. Immediately begin writing down impressions. Because skin will be used as an evaluation medium, and many natural essences do not easily wash off, even with soapy water, restrict the evaluations to about five or six per day, so as not to mix the essences on the skin and contaminate the evaluation results. Use the arms, wrists, hands and fingers as potential spots on which to drop essences for evaluation. Remember to sniff *gently*. Don't suck up the air like a vacuum, instead slowly and gently wave your scented hand or scent strip or bottle under your nose.

"Waft! Don't draft!" *Jeanne Rose, Aromatherapist, NBP,* *during an interview in December 2009*

  The evaluation exercise will help in remembering this essence when they are smelled again. It is a good idea to evaluate each essence at the dilutions listed for the trial evaluations for this book ~ 1%, 10% and 20% ~ to get a better understanding of how dilution ratios can affect the finished perfume.

Left Nostril/Right Nostril Evaluations

  There has been some controversy in recent years as to who first began utilizing the left/right nostril methodology of evaluating scent. This method of evaluating scent has been in use for decades, as Edward

Sagarin, author of *"The Science and Art of Perfumery"* wrote and published on the subject in 1945.

Olfactory Lateralization

According to an abstract submitted to the *Neuroscience Letters*, a study conducted upon human subjects showed a slight advantage in odor perception with right nostril as opposed to the left nostril: *"The analysis of the single odors of the Sniffin' Stick Test consistently confirmed higher intensity ratings for the right compared to the left nostril reaching a statistically significant difference for 10 out of 16 odors."*

What that means is that in reference to the intensity of a scent, the right nostril has an advantage over the left in scent detection. When it comes to a more hedonistic approach, another abstract in the *Oxford Journals* published in 1999 stated:

> *"Given that olfaction is predominantly ipsilateral in function, it was hypothesized that odor pleasantness evaluations may be accentuated by right nostril perception and that odor naming would be superior with left nostril perception. Results revealed that odors were rated as more pleasant when sniffed through the right nostril and named more correctly when sniffed through the left nostril."*

It is important to the study of Natural Botanical Perfumery to evaluate using left/right nostril methods if, as stated above, the left nostril is more accurate in identifying the essence being evaluated, and the right nostril perceives the odor as pleasant or unpleasant. To conduct an evaluation using this method, simply follow the instructions for conducting evaluations, and when sniffing, close off one nostril and sniff through the open nostril. The most important part of this type of evaluation is to accurately describe what is being smelled, and the differences in what is being detected between each nostril.

Describing Scent Effectively

It can be very difficult to describe scent effectively if the thought process attempts to rationalize or compare scent to another scent – a rose is a rose is a rose, but not really. While it's important to describe things as "agrestic or hay-like", "earthy, wet soil-like" and "floral", it's just as important to give the essences *life*. Try to suppress the rational brain or conscious thoughts while evaluating – use a more visceral approach, become meditative and write what is felt, give the essences emotion, personality, and vitality; use poetic prose to describe the scent experienced, set the stage, such as "it smells of the sun blazing through the frost of winter", or "it smells like the waxy red dashboard of a '64 Chevy Impala, and you know what *that* smells like because you've lain across it while drunk out of your mind", or its scent conjures thoughts of "moldy, home-made pickles with a glossing of high-octane ethanol and the pungent, cheesy essence of toe jam". In this way, the essences evaluated will imprint on the memory more personally.

If a perfumer is lucky enough to 'suffer' from the gift of synesthesia, this process becomes as easy as breathing. Synesthesia is "a neurological condition in which stimulation of one sensory or cognitive pathway leads to automatic, involuntary experiences in a second sensory or cognitive pathway". This means scent can be perceived as colors or flavors, or word associations immediately crop up that would not normally be used in describing the scent evaluated. Synesthesia has often been described as the feeling one has while using psychedelic drugs, where scent takes on vivid, vibrant color and movement.

What You and Your Nose Should Know

According to Avery Gilbert, author of "What the Nose Knows", "sniffing coffee beans does not 'refresh' the nose after prolonged smelling". The only way to clear or refresh the nose during evaluations is to stop the evaluations and get some fresh air.

How Do You Know if Your Essences Are the Real Deal?

In a nutshell, it is not always possible. Even with experience and cross-evaluations (evaluating the same material from several sources and countries of origin) a consumer may still be fooled. Adulteration of essential oils, and especially of rare, costly oils and absolutes such as hyacinth, jonquil, narcissus, jasmine, and Mysore sandalwood, is a common practice. Even the big perfume house suppliers offer absolutes that are "doctored", and what may be found is a natural compound, a blend of similar smelling aromatics professionally compounded to approximate the scent of *real*, rare absolutes, or it could be an outright synthetic.

Though natural compounds aren't truly adulteration as defined by a Natural Botanical Perfumer's standards, they are still misleading, and being sold unethically if the information of their origin and manufacture is not freely divulged.

One of the first red flags to watch for when purchasing the more rare aromatics is *cost*. If the price is too good to be true, beware! Also, if the aromatic being sold is something unusual, say tulip or cucumber blossom, it's either a fake or something like a Bach flower remedy extract, which will have no scent and is only appropriate for perfumery if utilizing the living essence and spiritual aspects of botanicals in perfumes.

The bigger issue is outright adulteration of natural aromatics to stretch the product and fatten the purses of the manufacturers. The bottom line is the supplier must be trusted. If an aromatic from a trusted supplier seems adulterated or altered somehow, ask them about it. Many suppliers are unaware they are being duped by their suppliers, but in a few rare instances, an end supplier will stretch the facts about an aromatic to suit their bottom line.

Arctander's *Perfume and Flavor Materials of Natural Origins* is the Natural Botanical Perfumer's bible, so to speak, in regard to all things related to Natural Botanical Perfumery. Arctander offers extensive descriptions in both the appearance and scent of essences used in perfumery; indispensable information for avoiding loading oneself with useless adulterated materials. This information may also be researched online.

One of the better websites for studying and becoming educated on the use and abuse of adulterants in the essential oil industry is Crop Watch by Tony Burfield at www.cropwatch.com.

Essence Evaluation Sample Worksheet

Date of Evaluation:

Name of Essence, Latin & Common	Violet leaf; viola odorata
Name of Supplier	Eden Botanicals
Country of Origin	France
Year/Month Purchased	04/01/08
Lot #/ID# from Supplier (if available)	Not available
Form, ie, essential oil, absolute, concrete, tincture, etc.	absolute
Intensity (1-10 scale)	medium
Actual Color	Olive green
Perceived Color	green
Dilution Ratio %	10%

Fruity	Floral	Woody	Green/ Herbal	Citrus	Amber/ Balsamic/ Resinous	Spicy	Medicinal/ Camphor	Earthy

1. Clarify or classify fragrance family; give detailed scent detection:
Green/herbal, slightly floral, cucumbery, watery, fresh, geranium leaf
2. Name secondary scents detected (ie lemon scent in frankincense, etc.):

Slightly salty, elements of cilantro and clary sage

3. Describe any scent memories associated with this essence:

Reminds me of cucumber salad, summer, hide and seek in the geraniums

	Strong	Weak	Same	Dry Down Notes/Secondary Notes
Evaluation at 15 minutes	√			*Cucumbery, green leaf, herbal*
Evaluation at 30 minutes	√			*Salty notes, green leafy presence*
Evaluation at 1 hour			√	*Has kind of a breathy, cilantro leaf like essence*
Evaluation at 2 hours		√		*Honeyish, slight saltiness, green herbal*
Evaluation at 3 hours		√		*Diminished green and white floral*

Evaluation at 6 hours		√	*Almost no scent left*
Evaluation at 12 hours		√	*Gone*
Evaluation at 24 + hours		√	*Gone*

Notes:

Very strong start with the high green leafy notes dominating, cucumbery, watery aspects prevalent, and a strange saltiness that seems like it might work well with an oceanic or clean, fresh, floral formulation; has decent tenacity for a top note

Supplemental Scent Vocabulary

Describing scent is not an easy task. The following descriptors for scent are presented as a starting point for developing an in-depth method of describing scent.

Aldehydic, agrestic (rustic, rural), ambery, animalic (furry, fecal), balsamic (bitter/ tannic = myrrh resin, opoponax), balsamic (sweet = benzoin), citrusy, clear, cloying, damp, dark, dry, earthy, fatty, floral, ferny, forest, fruity, fungal, green, herbal (rosemary, sage, lavender), high, honey (sweet, creamy, musky), leathery, medicinal (camphoraceous), metallic, minty, mossy, muddy, musky, oceanic, oily, piney, powdery, pungent, salty, smoky, spicy (hot = black and pink pepper, clove, cinnamon), spicy (green = coriander seed, coriander leaf), spicy (sweet = cardamom, nutmeg, allspice), tobacco-like, waxy, wet, woody.

Continued Olfactory Training

Another exercise which is important for reinforcing evaluations is the Twenty-A-Day exercise. Randomly select twenty diluted essences from the palette and without looking at the labels drop a single drop of each essence onto a scent strip or sniff straight from the dilution bottle, and attempt to guess what the essence is. Write the name of what is perceived on a piece of paper, and at the end of twenty evaluations, compare the answers to the essence's label. Mark those guessed incorrectly and tally up how many are correct and divide it by twenty (the total number of essences evaluated) – the resulting number is the percentage of correct answers. For example, if there are 15 correct, dividing 15 by 20 will give 0.75, which is the same as 75%. This is a great daily exercise to help strengthen the perfumer's ability to quickly identify scent.

CHAPTER 6

Journaling ...

Journaling perfume into existence is an important part of creating perfume. A journal is where perfume thoughts or ideas are kept; it's where the apprentice perfumer dips his or her toe, and then then slowly immerses into the pool of inspiration. It is where the very bones of perfumery creation begin.

No one ever knows from where a perfume inspiration will come – it may arise while driving to and from work in heavy traffic, or while in the shower, grocery shopping, during meditation, or even during sleep, dreaming perfume into existence. It is important to write down the ideas as soon as possible a great fear of a perfumer, as with many artists, is letting an idea go because there was no place to write it down, or we naively placate ourselves with the thought that because it was such a great idea, we are sure to remember it. That is usually not the case.

Journaling is very different than simply writing down formulations. Journaling is writing down thoughts and ideas freestyle. Journaling dedicates the words on the page to the perfumer's heart, and is best done on paper with a pen or pencil rather than on a computer. The tangibility of a journal, something which can be tucked into a handbag or briefcase and written in while the moment of inspiration arises, is of utmost importance. A journal is real; it can be touched, written upon, and coveted much more readily than a computer document.

This is something that is important in all the arts – the accessibility of documenting ideas as they come. Writers carry notebooks, painters carry small sketchbooks, and photographers carry cameras – all a means of documenting and preserving an artistic idea to be fleshed out later.

Be sure to use a dedicated journaling notebook(s) and not a formulation notebook or evaluation notebook. This is important because the journal is the well of inspiration and fussing it all up with eval notes and formulation trials will only distract from the purpose of journaling. It is a diary of the scented heart.

Transferring brief notes from an evaluation is okay if some inspiration or idea on blending from certain parts of an evaluation comes to mind. Tape scent strips with a quick trial to the journal to help better remember the core of the idea. Quick trials are the "let's see how this works" experiment of placing a drop of one or two essences onto a scent strip to serve as a guide for a perfumed idea or inspiration. These are not worked out trials, but rough sketches.

Many have asked the questions: how can scent be described? If it is an art form, in which category does it fall? Two-dimensional, such as film, or 3-dimensional as in theater and dance? Or does it fall into forms of prose or poetry? Perfumer Andy Tauer has coined a term which he uses to describe his perfumes, basically quantifying the art form. He calls it "Immersive Sculpture". By his own definition, Immersive Sculptures are, "Artistic perfumes that go beyond a simple scent. They are like sculptures, multidimensional, and they change their shapes and forms; artistic perfumes are immersive in the sense that you can step into them, experience them from inside, unify with them . . . More than just a fragrance [line], but rather like a second body forming around you."

CHAPTER 7

Apprenticeship …

Scales

A digital scale is a must when creating larger volumes of perfume concentrate. The accuracy of measurement is much higher when using a scale as opposed to using droppers. For example, a drop of distilled water weighs 0.025 grams; a drop of organic grain alcohol weighs 0.015 grams, and a drop of rosemary essential oil weighs 0.018 grams using the same size dropper and a digital scale which weighs to 0.001. Utilizing a scale which weighs at a higher weight, to $1/100^{th}$ (0.01), is sufficient. The difference at $1/1000^{th}$ (0.001) is negligible in larger volumes, but useful in illustrating the subtle differences in the weights of different fluid elements, and very useful for accurate single drop weights and conversions. Essential oils, as well as many other fluid raw materials used in natural perfumery, are measured by weight, not by volume, when they are packed for sale. The specific gravity, for which information can be found on the Material Safety Data Sheets provided by the supplier, indicates the weight of the raw material. For example, the molecular weight, or specific gravity, of rosemary essential oil contained within a one fluid ounce bottle is 0.9143 ounces.

The larger, higher capacity scales are the most desirable for large-scale perfume making endeavors. Have on hand at least two scales, one which weighs amounts between 0.01 grams to 1000 grams, and one which weighs down to $1/1000^{th}$, at 0.001 to the highest capacity you can obtain. The scale which weighs down to $1/1000^{th}$, 0.001, is to be used for dropper to weight conversions, and the larger scale capacity, the $1/100^{th}$ or 0.01, and up to 1000 grams, is used for converting from small batch capacity to large batch capacity, in the neighborhood of liters. *1000g = approximately 35 fluid ounces

Graduated Cylinders & Other Tools

Graduated cylinders are the easiest to use as the calibrations of some of the cylinders on the market are set at 0.1ml increments. A decent collection of graduated cylinders would include several of each in 10ml, 50ml, 100ml, 250ml and 500ml increments.

Dental tools, clay carving tools, nail kit tools, or even small, clean, unused flat-head screwdrivers are useful for scraping sticky and resinous materials from their bottles or jars. These tools can be obtained inexpensively at a laboratory supply store, an art or craft store, department store, auto parts store, or through Ebay.

Large apothecary bottles, flip-top rubber cork bottles, wine bottles, and vintage or antique *clean* perfume or factice bottles are crucial to creating large volumes of perfume, or when creating tinctures, evulsions and infusions.

Diluting by Volume and Weight

During the beginning portion of this manual, you learned to create dilutions using drops. Learn to convert the drops to milliliters or grams in order to make larger batches of dilutions. A milliliter of water weighs 1 gram; however other fluids may not due to their specific gravity

Milliliters

A ten percent dilution ratio (10%) using milliliters as the measure, with a total end product of 10mls would require one milliliter of fragrant material (eo, absolute, resin, concrete, etc.) to nine milliliters diluent (ethanol, oil) for a ratio total of *ten milliliters*. *A full ounce of a ten percent dilution (30mls)* would be made using three milliliters of fragrant material to twenty-seven (27) milliliters of diluent.

This is how the problem of dilutions in milliliters is worked out: let's say, for example, we are making 30mls (one ounce by volume) of dilution at 3%; convert the percentage to a decimal (0.03) and multiply 0.03 x 30mls, which gives .9mls; then subtract (30 – .9) to gives 29.1 – use .9mls of raw material to 29.1mls of diluents (alcohol/oil) for a final 30mls of a 3% dilution. A 6% dilution with a final total of 30mls would be worked out in this manner: 0.06 x 30mls = 1.8; 30 – 1.8 = 28.2; 1.8mls raw materials to 28.2mls diluents for a total of 30mls at 6% dilution.

Volume (30 mls = 1 fluid ounce)

Dilution Ratio %	Raw Material	Diluent
5.00%	1.5 mls	28.5 mls
10.00%	3 mls	27 mls
15.00%	4.5 mls	25.5 mls
20.00%	6 mls	24 mls
25.00%	7.5 mls	22.5 mls
30.00%	9 mls	21 mls
35.00%	10.5 mls	19.5 mls
40.00%	12 mls	18 mls
45.00%	13.5 mls	16.5 mls
50.00%	15 mls	15 mls

To make 5mls of a 10% dilution, calculate it in this manner:

Convert 10% to a decimal: 0.10

Multiply decimal by total amount of finished dilution desired (5mls): 0.10 x 5mls = .5

Subtract results of the above equation from total amount of finished dilution desired (5mls): 5mls - .5 = 4.5mls

Blend dilution at this ratio: .5mls raw materials to 4.5mls diluents (alcohol/oil) = 5mls at 10% dilution

Grams

There are 28.4 grams in a dry ounce. Conversion is done in much the same way as milliliters. Use gram weight calculations when making dilutions of sticky, resinous or solid raw materials. For example, to make a 3% dilution of Siam benzoin absolute, convert the percentage to a decimal (0.03) and multiply the dilution ratio (0.03) by the total number of grams (28.4g); 0.03 x 28.4g = .852g; then subtract the sum of this equation from 28.4g (28.4g - .852g = 27.548). Using a gram weight scale that weighs to 0.01 (1/100th) eliminate the 1000th's place in this equation (.852g would be .85g, and 27.548g would be 27.55g rounded up).

3% dilution in one ounce (28.4g) by weight

0.03 x 28.4g = .852g

28.4g - .852g = 27.548g

Final dilution:

28.4g – 27.55g = .85g

.85g raw material to 27.55g diluents = 28.4g (one ounce by weight) of a 3% dilution

Weight (28.4 grams = 1 ounce by weight)

Dilution Ratio %	Raw Material	Diluents
5.00%	1.42 g	26.98 g
10.00%	2.84 g	25.56 g
15.00%	4.26 g	24.14 g
20.00%	5.68 g	22.72 g

25.00%	7.1 g	21.3 g
30.00%	8.52 g	19.88 g
35.00%	9.94 g	18.46 g
40.00%	11.36 g	17.04 g
45.00%	12.78 g	15.62 g
50.00%	14.2 g	14.2 g

Drops to Milliliters or Grams

When using a scale to compose perfume, convert the drop-by-drop evaluations or trials into milliliters or grams for larger batch compositions. Conduct calibration of drops to milliliters to grams using the droppers and scale(s) and glass lab ware (graduated cylinders, beakers, flasks). Don't rely upon a standard as all droppers are not made equally, nor will the amount of fluid dispersed by the dropper be the same. For example, and for the purpose of illustrating a point in this unit, the author conducted experiments using three types of droppers to reach the one milliliter volume mark and weighed the results on a 0.001 (1/1000ᵗʰ) gram weight scale. Using organic grain alcohol as the measured medium and a one milliliter medical use dropper (marked and calibrated at exactly 1ml), the one ml of organic grain alcohol *weighed* 0.829 grams and was attained at 28 drops. A dropper purchased from a laboratory supply store required 46 drops to reach the weighed milliliter level of 0.829 grams, and using a small dropper from a 5ml amber bottle required 57 drops to reach the milliliter to gram weight level. The specific gravity of an individual essence has an effect on the results of the experiments, as will the difference in weight between a diluted and undiluted material.

Tinctures or Evulsions?

In Steffen Arctander's textbook "Perfume and Flavor Materials of Natural Origin", he writes:

"A tincture is a prepared perfumery material, flavor material or pharmaceutical product. Tinctures can be considered alcoholic extracts of natural *raw materials; the solvent is left in the extract as a diluent. Consequently, tinctures are not exposed to heat during preparation. There is no general rule governing the strength of perfumery or flavor tinctures."*

Of ultrasonic extraction, he writes:

"Ultrasonic extracts are prepared flavor materials, or in a few cases, perfume materials. Several methods of extracting natural raw materials with the aid of supersonic sound vibrations have been described in scientific literature, and many extractors have been patented. A few European flavor and perfume material suppliers specialize in such extracts, e.g. Camilli, Albert et Laloue in Grasse, France. *It is claimed that this method:*
1) gives higher yields,
2) reduces the amount of solvent needed,
3) greatly improves the flavor or odor in the sense that they become more true to nature,
4) reduces the extraction time considerably,
5) makes possible an extraction with water or low-proof alcohol where this is otherwise not too effective.
. . . The finely ground raw material is suspended in the menstruum (solvent/alcohol) in the extractor. High-frequency vibration is applied, and in an amazingly short time, the drug is exhausted. Due to the better yield given by this method in comparison to ordinary extraction, the ultrasonic extracts are often cheaper in use than the old types of extracts. This method is particularly useful for extraction of flavors from sensitive (heat-sensitive) raw materials, e.g. coffee, spices, etc., but flowers and herbs are also treated by this method now, e.g., mimosa, *thyme, etc.*

Because the end-product of a tincture differs from a supersonic or ultrasonic tincture, we've redefined the terms to more accurately describe the procedures used to obtain the final raw material.

Tinctures are made by combining raw materials (herbs, seeds, grasses, resins, woods, etc.) with high proof grain or grape alcohol and allowing them to steep. Succussion, banging the container in which the tincture is held against one's hand can be used, though this cannot be considered in any way similar to using an ultrasonic.

Evulsions are made by combining raw materials as described in the tincturing process with high proof grain or grape alcohol, and then placing the container holding these materials into an ultrasonic unit for a length of time as to extract, or pull, scent (or flavor) from the raw material into the menstruum (alcohol). By definition, evulsion means to forcibly extract, or to pull out.

Many natural perfumers have used this method of extracting high quality perfumery ingredients from evulsing raw materials at home using ultrasonic devices, such as jewelry cleaners or tattoo equipment cleaners, to achieve evulsions which rival the quality of expensive absolutes. Smaller devices can be utilized in producing small batches of evulsions; larger capacities, in the 2L or higher range, are much more desirable. There are not, as yet, any standards for ratios of raw material to solvent in the production of evulsions for the Natural Botanical Perfumer, however, the following information will help in solidifying a basic understanding of the techniques which produce high quality evulsions.

Sample (small test batch):

Ratio	Solvent 190 proof org. grain alcohol	Raw Material	Extraction Time
1 to 1	50 grams	50 grams	Six hours
2 to 1	66 grams	33 grams	Six hours
3 to 1	75 grams	25 grams	Six hours
3 to 2	60 grams	40 grams	Six hours

Experiment with the ratios using the same raw materials to obtain the results you desire; for example, run a small test batch of powdered basil at the 1-1 ratio, another at the 2-1 ratio, and so on and so forth, and then perform evaluations for each resultant evulsion. Certain raw materials will need a longer extraction time (many hours; 40+) to obtain a useable end product. Roots and resins may require a longer extraction time, while delicate fresh flowers and leaves need less extraction time. Experiment, experiment, experiment!

Be sure to follow the operating instructions for your ultrasonic device to keep it in good working order and to avoid accidents. Fill the cavity with distilled water so that the water level rises to the top of the cavity when placing the container of material into the ultrasonic, or use the minimum fill line as a gauge and adjust if the water level rises up and out of the cavity. *Never run the ultrasonic with the water level lower than the minimum fill line.

Utilizing the chart above, determine the ratio of the experimental evulsion, pour the solvent into the bottle or jar (jars are preferred as the opening is much wider, which is helpful when using bulky raw materials) add in the raw material, close the jar tightly and place it in the water bath in the ultrasonic device. For the best results, allow the materials intended for evulsing to dry out or wilt. Too much water in the plant material can ruin an evulsion. Plug in the device and turn it on to the highest time allowed. Some devices can become hot when used for long periods of time. It is a good idea to allow it to cool down between sessions.

When the evulsion reaches the four hour mark (for the purpose of this experiment), remove the jar from the water bath, unplug the ultrasonic and pour out the water. Strain the raw materials from the jar using a mesh strainer, straining the fluid portion of the evulsion into a clean glass jar or bottle (use a funnel if necessary). Label the bottle of finished evulsion with the amount of raw materials to solvent, date of extraction, number of hours (or minutes) needed to finish evulsing, and then conduct an evaluation of the finished product. If the evulsion is weak, begin the process over using the first extraction results into which another batch of raw materials are added, and conduct the experiment again. This would be a 2X (or two times) extraction.

For larger batches of evulsions, simply increase the number of grams to ounces and proceed as instructed above. Infusions can be created in the ultrasonic device if it has a heating element. Using either oil or alcohol, create an evulsion blend as instructed and place the bottle into the water bath of the ultrasonic device and turn on the heat. Experiment with time limits and test the resultant infusion every few hours for strength of scent.

Always follow the instructions that arrive with the ultrasonic. Water levels within the cavity are important to maintain when the unit is in use. Improper utilization of the ultrasonic could result in a malfunction causing permanent damage.

Tinctures/Extracts

Tincture: *"a solution of alcohol or of alcohol and water, containing animal, vegetable, or chemical drugs"*

Extract: *"to separate or obtain (a juice, ingredient, etc.) from a mixture by pressure, distillation, treatment with solvents, or the like"*

Tinctures are typically produced in much the same manner as an evulsion extraction without the use of an ultrasonic device. Tinctures are a combination of raw materials and alcohol combined in a bottle or jar and left to age or mature over long periods of time. Raw materials and alcohol are blended in the same ratios used for evulsions, stored in a cool dark place and shaken occasionally until a maturation date is achieved – one week for potent smelling raw materials, one month, six months or a year for less potent materials, or difficult materials that don't easily give up their scent, such as orris root pieces. There are no set time frames for determining the end of maturation. It is entirely up to the perfumer's discretion as to how long a tincture is allowed to marry before straining; however, a general rule of thumb is 'the longer, the better'.

Extracts are often used in the production of flavoring materials, so it is important to use organic grape or grain spirits, or vegetable glycerin as the menstruum, and raw materials which are meant for use in food, such as cloves, cinnamon, cardamom, vanilla, dried fruit, coffee beans, teas, cacao beans, etc. Extracts are made in the same manner as tinctures and ultrasonic tinctures; however, their finishing time is determined by flavor rather than strength of scent. Extracts can be used as a scenting material in natural and botanical perfumery.

Succussion

Dr. Samuel Hahnemann, an 18th Century German physician, is credited with creating a method of blending materials called succession. Dr. Hahnemann is also credited with developing the basis of homeopathy.

Succussion is a method of blending two or more ingredients in a bottle or jar to create a finished product. In the case of a Natural Botanical Perfumer, the ingredients used will usually be a botanical or nature based (cruelty-free animal) fragrant raw material and alcohol or oil. Succussion has a potential spiritual aspect as well. Most homeopaths believe that succession allows the healing, spiritual substances held within the material to be released and concentrated into the menstruum.

To create dilutions or tinctures by succession simply measure the raw materials and alcohol or oil into a bottle or jar using the charts provided for evulsions and tinctures, close the bottle/jar and with one hand, repeatedly smack the bottle/jar against the palm of the other hand. Creating dilutions and tinctures this way also has a meditative effect on the "succusor" which may also add to the spiritual effects of the finished product.

Ultrasonic Maturation

One way in which to speed the maturation process of a finished perfume composition is through the use of an ultrasonic device. Natural Botanical Perfumes require about four weeks' time to reach the stage of maturation. This process can be expedited by putting a finished composition into the ultrasonic device (as instructed for creating evulsions). This method requires some experimentation on the part of the Natural Botanical Perfumer as to time frames in which to conduct the ultrasonic maturation process. Sonication, the process of using ultrasonic to create tinctures and mature finished perfumes, disperses and disrupts biological materials within the bottle, extracting it from the fragrant raw material and injecting it into the menstruum.

Experiment with a finished perfume composition by splitting the composition in half and placing one half into the ultrasonic device and allowing the other to mature without the use of sonication. Test the results daily and make notes of what is observed. This will provide an outline of the time required to expedite maturation.

Distillation for Hydrosols/Floral Waters/Hydrolats

Distilling your own raw materials is perhaps one of the more gratifying experiences of a Natural Botanical Perfumer. Creating the base ingredients which go into a finished perfume formulations guarantees both the authenticity of the materials used, and the integrity of the source. Hydrosols, or hydrolats, the distilled water portion of the steam distillation process, can be used extensively in eau de toilettes, eau de colognes, eaux fraiche and aftershaves as a substitution for plain distilled water. Some hydrosols are so intensely fragrant they can be used as light perfumes on their own. Often small amounts of essential oil are obtained, which can be siphoned, diluted and utilized in a perfume creation.

To distill for oil it is important that materials are chosen wisely as more than likely a small distillation unit will be utilized, one which can be used indoors as opposed to the larger, more sophisticated apparatuses which large-scale distillers use. Use materials which give high yield results. Citrus and herbs give the highest oil yield and are the easiest to distill. To distill for hydrosols the materials used should be as fresh as possible and can be derived from varying categories of plants – from citrus to woods, and even earth and clays. Desiccated plant materials make poorer quality hydrosols.

Copper al embics are the simplest type of distillation unit to purchase, with nearly all parts of the apparatus in place. Purchase safe plastic tubing or copper tubing to complete the cycle (water circulation and drainage of finished product into vessels). Iberian Coppers at **http://www.copper-alembic.com/** offer a wide variety of copper al embics for the home distiller, and include instructions how to distill for essential oil as well as eau de vie. For the purposes of demonstrating the process of distillation, a copper al embic will be discussed in this lesson.

The Process

Different raw materials require different distillation treatments. For example, some delicate flowers transfer their scent as a hydrosol more effectively via steam distillation by which they are separated from the water and held above the steaming water in an upper chamber of the al embic. Others, such as rose petals, perform better if they are water distilled, in other words, floating freely in the water chamber (retort) rather than held over the steam. Experiment with the flowers obtained utilizing both methods of distillation to find which is best for the flower in question.

In a copper al embic, the steam chamber is separated by a narrowing of the neck of the top portion of the devise where a copper colander-like disk, a separator, is fitted to hold the materials in the top portion. This copper colander device is included with the al embic. For the first experimental *steam distillation* batch, fill the lower chamber (retort) with purified water almost to the top (be sure to measure how much water that is put into this chamber as it is important to know when to stop the distillation process). Fill the upper chamber, the steam chamber, with the raw material to be steam distilled, the fresher the better, insert the separator and fit the top into the retort and seal with *rye flour paste. Set the al embic over the heating element (gas flame is preferable) with the heat turned off, and begin attaching the condensing unit (which also is included with the al embic purchase). The condensing unit consists of a copper tube which coils into a copper housing in which cool water will be circulated. Attach a hose to a continuous water source, such as the kitchen sink faucet, and attach another hose at the other end that empties the circulating water into a large 5 gallon container.

Attach a hose which collects the condensed steam (hydrosol/essential oil) and empties into a clean, sterilized bottle, or leave the opening to drip directly into a clean, sterilized bottle. Turn on the gas under the al embic and set it to its lowest setting. It may take an hour or so before anything begins dripping from the condensing tube/opening into the bottle. Be sure the circulating water is turned on and also set to run a very small amount of water around the condensing coils. The water through the circulating water hose should just trickle through. Stop the process when 1/3 to 2/3 of the water placed into the retort has condensed into the receiving bottle. It is feasible at this time to refresh the plant materials in the top of the al embic and re-distill the first batch of hydrosol by placing it back into the retort and running the process again. This concentrates the scent of the hydrosol.

Water distillation is done in exactly the same way as steam distillation, except the botanicals being distilled are placed into the retort and water is poured over the top leaving the top half of the al embic, the steam chamber, empty to accumulate steam. Be aware that some plant materials are much more heat-sensitive than others and can only be distilled at very low temperatures to yield a favorable product, while other botanicals (woods, resins) may require higher heat to release their essence into the hydrosol.

*Rye flour paste is rye flour mixed with a little water to create a paste. This makes an effective non-cracking seal.

Enfleurage & Maceration

Many fragrant flowers do not give up their scent easily to distillation and must be processed in another way. Tincturing or evulsing is an option but may not yield a suitable product. Prior to solvent extraction of absolutes, a technique developed in France called "enfleurage" was used to draw the delicate and lush scents from such flowers as jasmine and tuberose. Enfleurage simply means to saturate fat with the scent of the flower. Panes of glass in wooden frames would be spread with clean solid fat, usually of animal origin, and flowers would be placed on the fat and left for a day or two until all the scent had transferred from the flower to the fat. Then the process would be repeated until the fat was saturated with scent, at which point the product would now be called pomade. Some pomades went directly into production as solid perfumes, face creams or hair grease, while the rest would be mixed with a solvent, 95% alcohol, and agitated until the scent in the fat transferred to the alcohol creating an "absolute". The spent fat would then be used to make soap as it would still be very fragrant.

This same process can be applied by modern day Natural Botanical Perfumers to create their own pomades and absolutes, but it is recommended we use plant based solid fats, such as organic refined palm or coconut oil (coconut oil melts at temperatures over 75 degrees Fahrenheit). Large picture frames with glass panes can be easily purchased almost anywhere and used as the enfleurage plate, or use a large glass casserole dish and coat the bottom with clean plant fat. An abundant supply of fresh flower plant material must also be available. Depending upon the amount of fresh flowers available, this process can take a few weeks to complete.

Maceration is an ancient form of extracting scent from plants and was used on nearly all plant material, from flowers to spices to roots and grasses. Maceration is perhaps the easiest method of extracting scent from plant material. Maceration is typically done in warm oils, for which organic refined coconut oil is a perfect medium. Fill a wide mouthed glass jar with the botanical materials being extracted, pour enough warm coconut oil over the top to cover the botanicals, close the jar with a tight-fitting lid and set the jar into a warm water bath. Do not overheat! Overheating of the oil will cause the oil to turn rancid. Heat the oil just enough to keep it fluid. Set the jar in a sunny window and allow the sun's glow to gently warm the contents. Once the botanicals are wilted and spent, strain out the botanicals and refresh the oil with a new batch of botanicals. Repeat as many times as desired until the oil begins to smell fragrant. When finished, strain the oil into a clean, sterile jar and use the product in solid perfumes, body butters, balms, massage and bath oils.

Macerations can also be purified to create an "absolute" by pouring the oil into 95% alcohol and shaking vigorously a few times a day, allowing the mixture to marry for a few weeks. Attempt to prevent the fat from solidifying during this process by occasionally warming in a water bath or placing the container in a sunny window. When ready to separate, pour the mixture into a bowl and freeze it for a few hours until the coconut fat solidifies. Carefully pop the frozen fat disk out of the bowl and strain the absolute into a clean, sterile bottle. Label accordingly. Save the coconut fat for use in solid perfumes, body butters or soap.

Oil-based and Solid Perfume Making

Many Natural Botanical Perfumers do not have access to neutral grain spirits and must rely upon oil as their perfume menstruum. Creating perfume in oil is done the same way as alcohol-based perfumes, with one important exception: more raw materials are necessary in the formula to give the perfume diffusivity. Oil tends to mute and hold down the notes of a perfume, but the advantage to this is that the perfume has a longer skin-life.

Oil- and solid-based perfumes are not graded in the same way as alcohol-based perfumes; in other words, there are no oil parfums or extraits, though one can argue this point, and no eaux, as these require water.

Sample Concentration for Oil-Based Perfume

	Perfume Concentrate	Oil Menstruum
Heavy	25% to 30%	70% to 75%
Medium	20% to 25%	75% to 80%
Light	18% to 20%	80% to 82%

Formulate the oil- and solid-based perfume concentrate as instructed in "Advanced Composition Techniques" further in this manual; for oil-based composition, use the chart above to determine the amount of perfume concentrate to oil menstruum. For solid-based perfumes, the following chart offers guidelines.

Sample Concentration for Solid-Based Perfume

	Perfume Concentrate	Oil Menstruum	Beeswax/Floral Wax
Heavy	25.00%	50.00%	25% (20% beeswax to 5% floral wax)
Medium	20.00%	55.00%	25% (20% beeswax to 5% floral wax)

Light	15.00%	60.00%	25% (20% beeswax to 5% floral wax)

Floral waxes, once a nearly useless by-product of the production of absolutes, are now being utilized in solid perfumes and soaps with optimal results. Floral waxes are inexpensive alternatives to more costly absolutes, offering nearly identical scent results, albeit somewhat weaker.

Melt the beeswax and/or floral wax in a stainless steel pot over boiling water (a bain marie), or melt the waxes in a microwave in a microwave-safe bowl. Keep careful watch over the melting waxes as they can burn and ruin the scent of the finished perfume. It is easier to incorporate the oil into the waxes if the oil has been warmed first. Warm the oil portion of the perfume in a bain marie or in the microwave, slowly pour the oil into the waxes and continue to stir until well incorporated. Use the dental or carving tools or a stainless steel spoon to stir the solid perfume base. Allow the solid perfume base to cool and solidify slightly, a light opaqueness in the appearance of the base will indicate the cooling; add in the perfume concentrate by drops, stirring constantly to incorporate. If at any time the solid perfume base begins to harden before all the perfume concentrate has been incorporated, place the container into a bowl or pan of hot water until the base reaches a consistency that can be stirred. Once all the perfume concentrate is incorporated into the solid perfume base, pour the solid perfume into slip-top tins, decorative tins or into a single tin for ageing. Do not at any point overheat either the base oil or waxes or it will result in a rancid smelling end product.

If the perfume concentrate is blended into the solid base when it is too hot, some of the scent will be lost to evaporation. It is important to maintain a stable level of heat to accomplish the tasks of melting and blending, along with providing a cool enough menstruum so as not to evaporate the perfume concentrate.

Compounding Fragrance for Soap, Butters, Scrubs, Balms & Massage Oils

Unlike compounding strictly for perfumery, compounding for body care products is done using whole raw materials or slightly diluted in oil raw materials. In other words, little or no dilution of the materials is required prior to compounding or composing the scent portion of these products. Soap in particular requires a bit more of the whole raw material than the butters, balms or oils as the process of saponification, the process by which oil and sodium hydroxide become soap, destroys a noticeable portion of the scenting materials. It is recommended that between 10 and 15 mls of perfume compound per one pound of soap is used to create a richly scented *savon parfume*.

Butters and balms require just a bit less scenting material per pound of oils, in the range of 8 to 10 mls. Massage and bath oils require even less, somewhere in the range of 3 to 5 mls per pound of oil.

Since this isn't a manual specific to soap, butter, balm, or bath and massage oils, only basic instructions for creating these products will be presented. Please read this entire chapter before attempting to create any of the products described here.

Formulate or compound the fragrance base for these products in the same manner as perfume formulation, conducting trial studies and remembering to compound the raw materials in their whole or near-whole form.

Soap Making 101

The most important lesson taken into consideration in learning botanical soap making is safety. Handmade soap, from cold process to hot process, is made using sodium hydroxide, commonly known as lye. Lye is a caustic chemical typically used to clear clogged drain pipes and is a major component in oven cleaners.

A basic list of safety gear includes:

Eye goggles

Disposable paper face masks

Gloves

Long-sleeved shirt

Bottle of apple cider vinegar

Running tap water or a big bottle of purified water

All these safety items must be present during the soap making process, and utilized whenever necessary.

Tools

A large *steel* pot (not aluminum, not Teflon coated, not cast iron)

Two wooden spoons

1 plastic scraping spatula

Small plastic bowl

10 ml graduated cylinder

Measuring cups

Digital kitchen scale

Heavy duty plastic pail or bucket

Cooking thermometer

Parchment paper

Box to use as a mold, can be cardboard, an old dresser or desk drawer, or a plastic storage box

Sharp, thin knife for cutting soap

Hand or stick blender (optional)

Raw Materials

Olive oil

Cocoa butter

Coconut oil

Sodium hydroxide (lye)

Distilled water

Perfume compound

Processing Cold Process Soap

The first thing to do, even before outfitting with the safety gear, is to prepare the soap mold. Line the box mold with pieces of parchment paper so that the entire inside of the mold is covered. Failing to do so will cause the soap to stick to the mold where there was no parchment paper and it will have to be pried from the mold.

Basic Soap Formulation:

200 grams olive oil*

227 grams cocoa butter
227 grams coconut oil
97   grams sodium hydroxide
 8   oz distilled water
10-15 mls perfume compound

     Gather all the safety equipment, tools and raw materials necessary for making soap. In the heavy duty pail or bucket, pour in the *measured* (in a measuring cup) distilled water which is called for in the soap recipe, and add the *weighed* (on the kitchen scale) sodium hydroxide/lye slowly, using one of the wooden spoons to stir and dissolve the lye. Wear the safety equipment during this stage! It is extremely important to blend the lye/water mixture in a room with good air circulation, and away from children and pets. Do not breathe in the fumes emanating from the mixture as it can cause serious damage to lung tissue. Wear the paper face mask! Once the lye has been completely dissolved, put the solution in a safe place to cool.

     At this point, the safety gear can be removed. *Weigh* the oils and butters individually in the small plastic bowl on the kitchen scale, pour the oils into the steel pot and set the heat under the pot on its lowest setting to just barely warm the oils. Melt the cocoa butter in a microwave or *bain marie* (double boiler) and add it to the warmed oils once it has melted. Overheating the oils and butter will cause the finished product to become rancid, so it is very important to heat at just above body temperature (around 100 to 105 degrees Fahrenheit).

     Measure the perfume compound in the graduated cylinder, and pour it into the small plastic bowl with a small amount, about 30 mls or so, of olive or other fluid vegetable oil, and blend well. *The 30 mls of olive oil or other fluid oil mixed with the perfume compound makes up for the deficiency in the base oil weights given above.

     Once the lye/water solution cools to about 100 degrees Fahrenheit, gear up in the safety equipment, and slowly pour the lye/water solution into the warm oils in the steel pot, using a wooden spoon to stir. Stir continuously for about 15 to 20 minutes, or use a dedicated hand blender, in which case it will take about 3 minutes to reach "trace".

Trace is a term describing the point at which the lye/water and oils are thoroughly blended and are ready to be poured into a mold. Before soap reaches trace, it goes through a "grainy" period, when the lye/water and oil solution takes on a grainy appearance. It means that trace isn't far off. When trace is reached, the soap will look like thin pudding and will leave a trail across the surface of the soap when drizzled off the wooden spoon. The soap will become thicker the longer it is stirred, and at some point will become too thick to pour, so it is important to first recognize trace, and second, pour before it becomes solid.

Just after the soap reaches trace, pour the pre-measured perfume compound and oil mixture from the small plastic bowl into the soap and stir thoroughly. Using the scraping spatula, pour and scrape the soap into the prepared mold and allow it to set and move on to wash all the equipment.

The soap must be kept warm. If it is a warm day, leave the soap out in the open to cure. If it is a cool or wet day, the soap may need to be popped into the oven (which is OFF), or place cardboard over the top and wrap with towels to retain the heat. The saponification process between the lye and oils will create a lot of heat. Maintaining that heat for as long as possible is necessary for proper curing.

After 24 hours in the box mold, pop the soap out (if it is hard enough), and cut into bars, and set them on parchment paper to dry and further cure. The curing process takes about 3-4 weeks.

Basic Butter and Balm Formulations

So what's the difference between butter and a balm? A butter is made using plant butters and liquid plant oils; cocoa butter, mango butter, olive butter, shea butter and many more, while balms are made using some butters and liquid plant oils with the addition of *waxes, either plant or beeswax. Common plant waxes are soy wax, carnauba wax and candelilla wax. Small amounts of floral waxes can also be included, but be careful when using them as they are very waxy and leave a sticky residue on the skin if too much has been processed into the balm.

Tools for butter and balm making include:

Double boiler or bain marie

Digital kitchen scale

Small plastic bowl

10 ml graduated cylinder

Sterilized containers with lids

Stick blender or hand mixer (optional)

Assortment of butters, oils and plant waxes

Perfume compound

*Per Jeanne Rose, a 'balm' made of beeswax is a cerate; a balm can be any type of skin care application. Calling it a balm is a preference of the person creating the 'balm'.

Again, as in the soap making process, overheating of the oils and butters will cause them to become rancid more quickly than usual. Presented below is a *basic butter recipe*. Please note that these recipes can be modified to suit tastes and texture preferences. Prepare the sterilized containers and leave them nearby with the lids off. It is important to move quickly during the last stage of the process to get the butter into the container before it solidifies.

Simple Butter Formulation:

300 grams of butters (shea, olive, almond, cocoa, mango, hemp seed, kokum, etc.)
150 grams liquid plant oil (olive, almond, jojoba, borage, coconut, neem, etc.)

8 – 10 mls perfume compound

Melt the butters on very low heat in a double boiler or bain marie. Once all the butters are melted, set a timer or watch the clock and wait for 20 minutes to pass. Continuing to heat for this length of time will prevent the butter from becoming grainy when it cools. After 20 minutes of low, slow heating, remove the melted butters from the heat and allow the mixture to cool to about the point just before it wants to solidify again – around 110-115 degrees Fahrenheit, and add in the liquid plant oils, mix well, and pour in the perfume compound, again, mixing well.

At this stage pour the butter into the containers, or, if a fluffier, more airy butter is preferred, whip it with the stick blender, whisk or hand mixer for just a few moments (watch for it to solidify as it will do so quickly), then pour into the containers. If the butter solidifies before it is poured into the containers, set the butter back into the warm water bath of the double boiler or bain marie to just melt the butter from the sides of the bowl, then begin whipping until it reaches a pourable consistency and quickly pour it into the containers.

A Simple Butter Scrub Formulation:

300 grams of butter (shea, olive, almond, cocoa, mango, hemp, kokum, etc.)
 75 grams liquid plant oil (olive, almond, jojoba, borage, coconut, neem, rosehip, etc.)
*100 grams organic unrefined sugar
 8 – 10 mls perfume compound

Whip with a stick blender if using a soft butter, such as shea, mango, hemp or kokum, and slowly pour in the liquid oils, then the sugar, and last, the perfume compound. Mix thoroughly and spoon the butter scrub into containers. If the butter is solid, such as cocoa butter, melt over a bain marie and continue as instructed for soft butter scrub.

*Add more or less sugar – for a creamier scrub, use less sugar, for a thicker, denser scrub, use more sugar and heavier butters (cocoa). It is option to add whole or *powdered herbs and flowers such as rose petals, lavender buds, poppy seeds, citrus peel, rosemary herb, etc. Also substitute the sugar with salt, but remember that salt will cause burning and itching if applied to broken skin.*

A Simple Balm Formulation:

290 grams of butters
150 grams liquid plant oil
10 grams wax
8 – 10 mls perfume compound

Melt the wax first, add in the butters and proceed as described for butter making. Skip the whipping process and pour the balm directly into containers.

Massage & Bath Oils

Scented body oils are perhaps the easiest of all the body care products to create, plus they offer instant gratification for the impatient. The best oils for making massage oil are *organic, unrefined or lightly refined of the best quality* sweet almond, jojoba, fractionated coconut or apricot kernel. Sunflower oil is also good as an additive to massage oils, but not as a main component as it is thicker and "sticks" more readily during massage. The best oils to use for the bath are "thinner" oils, those oils which break apart and disperse throughout the water more readily. Safflower and fractionated coconut, as well as olive and jojoba, work best.

Tools to create massage & bath oils are:

Medium mixing bowl with spout

Sterilized containers with caps or lids

Digital kitchen scale

10 ml graduated cylinder

Wooden mixing spoon

Assortment of liquid plant oils

Perfume compound

Basic Massage Oil Formulation:

1 lb single or blended oils from list above
3 – 5 mls perfume compound

Weigh the oils in the mixing bowl on the kitchen scale, then add in pre-measured perfume compound and stir thoroughly with the wooden spoon. Pour into sterilized containers and cap.

Bath Oil Formulation:

1 lb safflower oil or blend of safflower and other liquid oils which best disperse in water
3 – 5 mls perfume compound

Follow instructions for making massage oil.

Creating Perfume

In this author's opinion, the best perfume composition modality to learn by is the Jean Carles Method outlined here, originally published as reprinted articles from **Recherches**, 1961, 1962, 1963, into the coffee table book **Perfume** by William Kaufman, *p. 1974*. Many famous Natural Botanical Perfumers over the past few decades have utilized Mr. Carles methods in an autodidactic setting in order to perfect their art. According to Carles, perfumers formulated in a disorganized manner, hoping to get lucky with the end result. Mr. Carles Method of perfume formulation helps a beginning perfumer better understand essence ratios and precisely how essences will work together.

Vertical & Horizontal Trial Studies

Trials and studies are tests performed by blending together essences to create a new scent that will be used in a perfume. A vertical study is utilized when contrasting essences categorized in different parts of perfume (head/top, heart/middle and bottom/base), or essences of different volatility levels. These studies are helpful in better understanding how different essences from different categories work together to create a harmonious accord.

Begin the study by dropping one drop of each essence of the 1% dilution strength onto a scent strip. Be sure to mark the type of study (vertical or horizontal), and the trial study number (Trial #1, Trial #2, etc.) when filling out the trial studies' worksheet. Starting with a new scent strip, begin the study again using the 10% dilutions, and again, with a new scent strip, begin the study using the 20% dilutions.

Vertical Study	Trial #1
Bergamot 1%	1 drop
Jasmine 1%	1 drop
Patchouli 1%	1 drop

Expand on these trials by using essences of different ratios. For example:

Vertical Study	Trial #2
Bergamot 10%	1 drop
Jasmine 10%	1 drop
Patchouli 10%	1 drop

Vertical Study	Trial #3
Bergamot 20%	1 drop
Jasmine 20%	1 drop
Patchouli 20%	1 drop

Continue with these studies until all possible combinations, including increasing and decreasing the number of drops, has been exhausted. A clear idea of how essences work together, do not work together, or are manipulated by ratios will be obtained through these trial studies.

A horizontal study is utilized when comparing essences from the same category or of the same volatility level.

For the horizontal studies, proceed as described in the vertical studies, beginning with one drop of each essence of the same dilution strength on a scent strip, evaluating the results and writing down impressions in a notebook. Continue the horizontal studies in the same manner as described in the vertical studies until all possible combinations have been exhausted.

Horizontal Study Base Notes			
Patchouli 1%	Ambrette Seed 1%	Tobacco 1%	Himalayan Cedar 1%

At 10%

Horizontal Study Base Notes			
Patchouli 10%	Ambrette Seed 10%	Tobacco 10%	Himalayan Cedar 10%

At 20%

Horizontal Study Base Notes			
Patchouli 20%	Ambrette Seed 20%	Tobacco 20%	Himalayan Cedar 20%

And mix the ratios:

Horizontal Study Base Notes			
Patchouli 20%	Ambrette Seed 10%	Tobacco 1%	Himalayan Cedar 20%

And heart notes:

Horizontal Study Heart Notes			
Rose Otto 1%	Jasmine Sambac 1%	Cananga 1%	Clove 1%

At 10%

Horizontal Study Heart Notes			
Rose Otto 10%	Jasmine Sambac 10%	Cananga 10%	Clove 10%

At 20%

Horizontal Study Heart Notes			
Rose Otto 20%	Jasmine Sambac 20%	Cananga 20%	Clove 20%

And mix the ratios:

Horizontal Study Heart Notes			
Rose Otto 1%	Jasmine Sambac 10%	Cananga 20%	Clove 1%

And head notes:

Horizontal Study Head Notes			
Bergamot 1%	Orange 1%	Lime 1%	Violet Leaf 1%

At 10%

Horizontal Study Head Notes			
Bergamot 10%	Orange 10%	Lime 10%	Violet Leaf 10%

At 20%

Horizontal Study Head Notes			
Bergamot 20%	Orange 20%	Lime 20%	Violet Leaf 20%

And mixed ratios:

Horizontal Study Head Notes			
Bergamot 10%	Orange 20%	Lime 1%	Violet Leaf 10%

Trial studies can be time consuming and exhausting, but are well worth the time and effort expended as the information acquired through these studies is invaluable to future perfumery endeavors.

What Do I Do With All These Trial Studies When I'm Finished Formulating?

Good question! Most perfumers have in their perfume studios a big bottle specific to this purpose. Perfume factice bottles, one liter corked bottles, pretty decorative bottles, whatever is on hand that will hold the hundreds, if not thousands, of trials to be conducted over the years. At the end of a formulating session, pour the trials and failed formulations into the studio bottle with a big label on it that reads, *Milles*

Fleurs. At the very least it will be quite the conversation piece, and it may even smell nice. When the bottle becomes too full, repurpose the contents into room or linen spray or bottle it up with a vintage poison label and give it away to friends and family at Halloween.

Why Do I Work With Diluted Materials?

Another good question! There are several reasons a beginning perfumer should work with dilutions, one being the cost of materials is reduced when utilizing them in dilutions. For example, a one ounce bottle or rose otto is priced at around $400 USD. It may not be feasible for a beginning student of perfumery to purchase an entire ounce of rose otto, instead opting to purchase a sample size at $30 USD per two milliliters. In order to have enough material to work with, it is necessary to dilute the two milliliters of rose otto to between 3% and 5%, yielding an increase of useable material to about an ounce (30 mls). Dozens upon dozens of trial studies can be completed utilizing one ounce of diluted rose otto. Another reason to use dilutions is due to the nature of their form. Most raw materials do not reflect their true aroma until they are diluted, as they are in a concentrated form, i.e. essential oil, absolute, concrete, CO_2 extraction, etc. The closest analogy to explain this would be the Frozen Orange Juice Analogy. Frozen concentrated orange juice must be diluted prior to consuming as it is a concentrated, thus intensely flavorful, and perhaps unpleasant, form of orange juice. The dilution ratio is somewhere around 25% to 30% to create a useable product. The same theory applies to many perfumery raw materials.

Trial Studies

Conduct a vertical trial study and a horizontal trial study using any combination of essences. Use the trial study worksheets provided in the companion workbook. Circle the trial study number which is the best balanced.

1. Proportions do not always translate. For example, a 1:1:1

proportion usually doesn't smell the same as a 20:20:20 proportion.

2. Sometimes the essence in higher percentage is buried under the essence or essences of lower percentage.

These trials will demonstrate the work involved in Natural Botanical Perfume composition.

Sample Vertical & Horizontal Trial Study Worksheet

Vertical _____ √_____ Horizontal _____
Date of Study _____

	Essence	Essence	Essence
	Lime	Jasmine	Patchouli
Dilution ratio %	1.00%	1.00%	1.00%
Notes: no lime at all, vague whiff of jasmine, hint of patchouli, after an hour the lime and jasmine create a soft, powdery melange almost like lavender			

Vertical _____ √_____ Horizontal _____
Date of Study _____

	Essence	Essence	Essence
	Lime	Jasmine	Patchouli
Dilution ratio %	1.00%	10.00%	1.00%
Notes: jasmine seems medicinal in this, harsh, not very nice at all; not really getting the other essence			

Vertical _____√_____ Horizontal _____
Date of Study _____

	Essence	Essence	Essence
	Lime	Jasmine	Patchouli
Dilution ratio %	1.00%	1.00%	10.00%
Notes: wet cardboard, then powdery notes; nothing really asserts itself in this combination			

Vertical _____√_____ Horizontal _____
Date of Study _____

	Essence	Essence	Essence
	Lime	Jasmine	Patchouli
Dilution ratio %	10.00%	1.00%	1.00%
Notes: smells like citrusy bathroom cleanser, with a little bit of lavender undertone; actually quite nice, but after an hour, all that's there is the lime			

Vertical _____ Horizontal _____

Date of Study _____

	Essence	Essence	Essence
	Lime	Jasmine	Patchouli
Dilution ratio %	1.00%	10.00%	10.00%
Notes: boring; bit of lime and that's it			

Intuitive & Creative Methods of Perfumery

After spending some time with the raw materials, and better learning their character, a naturally progressing ability to just know when a formulation worked out in your head or on paper will work. Some perfumers develop this ability early on, others later, but regardless of when the intuitive groove is discovered, rest assured that some of the more intuitively developed formulations are also some of the finest. Quite a lot of your ability to formulate perfume well will come from intuition achieved through essence evaluation, and a perfume journal may be instrumental in building these intuitive abilities.

It is safe to say, however, that *there are few rules* when it comes to the method of formulation chosen by the individual Natural Botanical Perfumer. Even though there are few rules, the rules that should never be ignored are the very basic: *Learn all that is possible about the character of the essences with which you are working. That knowledge is gained through diligent study of the essences used in perfumery and how they interact with one another ~ essence evaluations and the Carles' Method of conducting trial studies are vital to this process.*

Frozen Orange Juice Analogy

All essences are concentrates, and many smell nothing like the natural state of the botanical from which they are retrieved *until* they are diluted. In this book, most of our botanical concentrates are diluted to 10%, but that is simply a standard applied to teaching *this* method of perfumery, also known as the French method. It is a choice, part of a well-developed perfuming style that will dictate what method each perfumer follows. Choosing to dilute the initial materials to 1%, 5%, 10%, 20% and variations according to the raw material used *and then choosing not dilute any further to grade the perfume* is perfectly acceptable. A perfumer will learn to dilute to a strength which suits his or her formulating style as they becomes more familiar with the raw materials. At some point in a perfumer's journey, formulating perfumes using essences diluted in ranges from 0% (100% non-diluted essence), to 0.1% will become the norm. All of these dilution rate choices will be made because the individual perfumer did the work which contributed to his or her vast knowledge of the raw materials' character. The English method of perfumery is one in which all the components of a perfume are built using whole materials then diluted and filtered later.

Keep in mind is that the finished perfume formulation created is not really finished until it ages. Oftentimes, ageing a composition will change its character from the original in such a way as to make it either better, or in some cases, worse.

According to an article written for the *Soap, Perfumery & Cosmetics Buyer's Guide & Cyclopaedia of 1938*:

When the English method is employed, the proportion of raw materials (i.e., essential oils, synthetics, natural absolutes, fixatives, etc.) should not exceed some 10 to 15 per cent of the quantity of solvent used. With the alternative method, a mixture is simply made of the various *alcohol tinctures.

The possible addition of water, which in the cheaper perfumes amounts sometimes to as much as 20 per cent, lends itself very readily to the precipitation of the less soluble bodies. In any case, filtration is essential, if it is desired, to obtain a really crystal-clear product.

The mode of filtration shows little variation. Filtering may be effected either through filter paper, or through one of the special mineral products that are now being offered. The latter are used in conjunction with such improved pieces of apparatus as the Seitz filter–this being a popular type on the Continent that may be obtained for use either with or without pressure.

After filtration has been properly carried out, a perfectly clear and brilliant solution should be obtained, **but unless the solution has been chilled prior to filtration***, there is still most likely to be a progressive precipitation over a period of months, particularly during cold weather. This is especially the case with certain synthetics, and also with perfume concretes that still contain traces of wax and other impurities. The latter are frequently soluble in essential oils and alcohol at normal temperatures, but are precipitated as soon as the temperature is lowered.*

An old trick of the trade, used in conjunction with the English method of compounding, is to dissolve the concentrate in three-quarters of the alcohol, plus any water that has to be incorporated. The perfume is then chilled, filtered, and subsequently the other quarter part of the alcohol is added. This, as one would expect, is a very effective guard against further precipitation.

It should be particularly emphasized that chilling is an **essential part** *of perfumery production, and a refrigerator adapted for the purpose should be installed in every factory.*

*diluted material

English Method of Compounding Perfume

Simply put, the English Method of Compounding Perfume is one which utilizes whole, undiluted raw materials in the formulation phase, wherein alcohol and water are added later to grade the perfume's strength.

French Method of Compounding Perfume

This is the dilution method at its finest. All perfumes are formulated utilizing diluted materials, perhaps with some addition of water, depending upon the intended strength of the finished product. The French Method may or may not require additional alcohol to grade the perfume.

Sample "Intuitive" Perfume Outline and Formulation Using Mixed Dilution Ratios

Journal Notes: the tea house downtown; dark and exotic, smoky and sweet, honey on the air, the sounds of people whispering in the corner, quiet laughter, someone playing guitar on the sidewalk outside, the soft, squishy pillows on the couch, the tall frosty glasses of honey-sweet jasmine green tea and lavender Earl Grey, ginger and cinnamon, sugared almond cookies.

Notes ~ tea, cabreuva, jasmine, lavender, vanilla, honey, ginger, clove, sandalwood, bergamot, cananga, white champa leaf

Trial #1

Note	Drops	Dilution
tea	20	5%
cabreuva	20	5%
jasmine	3	3%
lavender	1	10%
vanilla	2	10%
honey	1	aged tincture 3x
ginger	1	10%
clove	2	1%

sandalwood	1	10%
bergamot	5	10%
cananga	1	10%
white champa leaf	1	10%

Let's say we evaluate this formulation and find that the tea notes are lost and the clove note takes over, and the dry down is dominated by the vanilla, so we would adjust our formulation to perhaps look like this:

Trial #2

Note	Drops	Dilution
tea	25	5%
cabreuva	25	5%
jasmine	3	3%
lavender	1	10%
vanilla	1	10%
honey	1	aged tincture 3x
ginger	1	10%
clove	1	1%
sandalwood	1	10%
bergamot	5	10%
cananga	1	10%
white champa leaf	1	10%

Now let's say we discover the head notes are nowhere to be found, our opener is strictly ginger and that's it, but we want more of the beautiful floral orange of bergamot, we would restructure our trial, Trial #3 now, to include more bergamot, like so:

Trial #3

Note	Drops	Dilution
tea	25	5%
cabreuva	25	5%
jasmine	3	3%
lavender	1	10%
vanilla	1	10%
honey	1	aged tincture 3x
ginger	1	10%
clove	1	1%
sandalwood	1	10%
bergamot	10	10%
cananga	1	10%
white champa leaf	1	10%

Some of the elements chosen for a composition will require further dilution to master, for example, in the sample trials the tea absolute may require further dilution to 3%, or the clove to 0.5%. An easier way to adjust for these situations is to increase the amount of the trial sample. There will be some instances during formulating that will require the use of materials at very low dilutions for them to work effectively in the composition. When the formulation is complete, convert the drops to grams or milliliters and formulate for more volume.

Does Having a Great "Nose" Make One a Great Perfumer?

In a word: No. There are many accounts of fabulous noses, people who can pick a scent apart note by note and describe them in a way that makes one feel they smell the same essence *the nose* smells, who cannot formulate perfume at all. Conversely, not being able to accurately describe a scent or the inability to name a note in a perfume composition does not make one a "bad nose". Creating perfume is as much an intuitive talent as it is a calculated one.

Basic Instruction for Creating Base Compounds

Building bases can be an important part of a Natural Botanical Perfumer's style of creation. Not all Natural Botanical Perfumer's build bases, a combination of essences which mock or mimic certain other scents for which there are no perfect natural sources, i.e. leather, musk, ivy, lily, tea, etc. Not all bases mimic specific natural scents – some bases expand and perfect scents created entirely from the perfumer's imagination. Bases can also be referred to as accords. Bases are typically a combination of essences which, as a perfumer, can be used in more than one creation An example of a famous base is Guerlain's "Guerlainade", a sweet, sticky, vanilla base Guerlain uses (or used) in many of their more popular creations (Shalimar & Jicky in particular).

Not only do bases help with creating a perfume by offering a "short cut" to complete perfume compositions, it also creates brand or perfumer style definition to creations. The bases chosen to create can be top note bases, heart note bases, base note bases or accessory note bases. Bases are pre-formulated compositions of essences and/or tinctures and evulsions used to flesh out or define a perfume composition.

An example of a roughly sketched formulation utilizing a "base" might look like this:

Top Notes ~
bergamot

lime
cilantro
spearmint

Heart Notes ~
tea rose
frankincense

Base Notes ~
*vanilla base
ambrette
V. sandalwood

*The "vanilla base" might be a combination of a vanilla evulsion, vanilla CO2, tonka, Siam benzoin, clary sage absolute, saffron absolute and other aromatics which have been prepared in advance for use in several formulations. Amber formulations are one of the more common bases and quite a few NBP's utilize their own amber formulation in many of their compositions. This is a way to identify a perfumer's "mark" or "hand" in a blend.

Floral Base

Create a floral base utilizing the materials recommended in this book. Be sure to include only those materials/essences which are floral in nature or that expand and diffuse the florals in the composition. For example, a floral base might include the more common florals in a perfumer's palette; rose, jasmine and ylang-ylang. A very nicely rounded floral base can be achieved utilizing just these three florals. This would be considered a simple base. The base can be boosted and expanded by adding osmanthus for a darker toned floral base, or neroli for a fresher, greener floral base; clary sage absolute or lavender creates an herbal/floral base; tuberose a lush, creamy base. The possibilities are limitless.

Utilize at least FOUR florals and as many floral boosters as you like to build a floral base. Evaluate the results and trials, and note how this base can be used and interpreted in a perfume

Amber Base

Amber bases are a much discussed topic among Natural Botanical Perfumer's since nearly all (and quite possibly all) commercially produced ambers are made utilizing synthetic molecules, which leaves us, as Natural Botanical Perfumers, to learn to build our own.

Basic construct materials for amber bases are:

benzoin
labdanum
vanilla

To these we may add other essences which round out the composition and make our amber bases our own ~ essences such as:

clary sage absolute
rose otto
rose absolute
tonka
sandalwood
choyas
ambrette
frankincense
tolu balsam
Peru balsam
orris root
spikenard
patchouli
clove
cardamom

vetyver
myrrh
and on and on . . .

       Construct two different amber base accords, and add in a few essences not on the amber base accord list. Amber "types" are different scent profiles of a basic amber blend of benzoin, labdanum and vanilla, and adding other aromatics to create a "warm amber" with the addition of more vanilla, notes of honey and florals and earthy essences, or a "spicy amber" by adding cassia, clove, cardamom, ginger and other spices, or a "floral amber" by adding rose, jasmine, osmanthus, or tuberose; a "light amber" can be created by reworking the base to illuminate the labdanum over the benzoin and adding small amounts of sandalwood and frankincense, or a "dark amber" by adding oudh, indolic florals, patchouli, choyas, vetyver or cepes. Be creative.
       Evaluate the results and trials, and note how this bases can be used and interpreted in a perfume.

Chypre Base

       Chypres are created using oakmoss, the recently much maligned and irreplaceable oakmoss. The basic construct of a chypre base includes the following essences, with the main focus on the first *four ingredients:

*bergamot
*oakmoss
*ambrette
*labdanum (cistus)
vetyver
patchouli
sandalwood

To this basic construct, one can add the following modifying essences to create a chypre perfume or accord:

orange
rose
juniper
lemon
orris
clary sage
neroli
geranium
benzoin
clove
jasmine
ylang-ylang
caraway
galbanum

Simple Chypre formulation:

bergamot (more bergamot)
orange
rose
chypre base

Citrus Base

Citrus bases are used primarily as top notes in a blend, alone or in addition to other top note essences. Citrus bases are important in the creation of eau de toilettes, colognes, eaux fraiche and aftershaves.

Utilizing all or part of the citrus family essences in a perfumer's palette, create two bases for evaluation and describe how it might be used in a formulation.

Think *Neroli Cologne* by Czech and Speake; *Eau de Cologne* by Hermes; *Imperiale* by Guerlain; *Kolnisch Wasser* by Farina Gegenuber;

Zephyr by Shiseido.

Citrus Base 1 Woody ~
orange peel
lemongrass
ho wood (or rosewood)

Citrus Base 2 Floral ~
petitgrain
neroli
bergamot
pink grapefruit

Violet Base

Violet bases are tricky and require some rare and expensive elements in their creation, such as boronia and orris root. But with skillful additions to violet base, create a wide range of violet perfumes, or perfumes which include an authentic violet note, can be created.

Violet leaf absolute
cassie absolute
oakmoss absolute
orris (absolute, evulsion, or butter)
tuberose absolute
ambrette seed oil
rose de mai absolute
tonka absolute
almond extract
boronia absolute

Formulating Perfume on Paper

Perfume begins on paper. Before opening a bottle or waft a scent strip, the first order of building a perfume begins with the journal inspirations, where the bones of the formulation are written down in detail. Moving from a journal to an Excel spreadsheet or dedicated notebook is the next step, and this is where a formulation is worked out in detail.

Advanced Composition Techniques

Let's imagine that you wanted to build an amber perfume. Find those materials within the perfumer's palette which exude the 'amber' essence desired ~ cistus, vanilla, styrax/benzoin, beeswax. For a spicy Oriental amber perfume, add clove or cassia (heavily diluted, of course), cardamom or nutmeg; a warm amber perfume might include ingredients such as Himalayan cedar wood and rose in the heart; a cool amber perfume might be obtained by adding green or watery notes like violet leaf, coriander, galbanum or blue lotus. To find the right combination, perform trials.

Amber Inspired		
	Essence	**Dilution %**
head	bergamot	10.00%
	coriander	10.00%
heart	rose	10.00%
	ylang-ylang	10.00%
	lavender	10.00%

base	cistus	10.00%
	vanilla	evulsion
	styrax, (benzoin)	10.00%
	beeswax	evulsion

(Example of Perfume on Paper)

Trials

Let's look at our amber inspiration again with its base of cistus, vanilla, styrax, and beeswax. In order to achieve the correct percentage of each material in our base, we begin with our trials based on the Carles Method of perfume formulation. These trials can be performed on scent squares cut from acid free watercolor paper or in 5 ml dropper bottles. If scent squares are used, there is no clean-up. The bottles will require washing and sterilization when the trials are complete.

Further along in composition building, when the three accords are combined (head/top, heart/middle and base/bottom), blend them in the 5 ml dropper bottles and adjust the amount of each accord so there will be enough of the composition to formulate. To make these adjustments, multiply the trial drops by ten. For example, if the trial chosen to represent the perfume theme contained eight drops of vanilla and two drops of cistus, expand the amount by multiplying the original number of drops of each essence (8 d. vanilla and 2 d. cistus) by ten. This expanded trial would then include 80 drops of vanilla and 20 drops of cistus.

Use the same size droppers for all the trials.

Choose the two essences which best represent the desired result.

Amber Base	Trial #1	Trial #2	Trial #3	Trial #4	Trial #5
cistus	9 drops	8 drops	7 drops	6 drops	5 drops
vanilla	1 drop	2 drops	3 drops	4 drops	5 drops

Continue working the trials ~

Amber Base	Trial #6	Trial #7	Trial #8	Trial #9
vanilla	9 drops	8 drops	7 drops	6 drops
cistus	1 drop	2 drops	3 drops	4 drops

Leave off the 5/5 trial in this set because it has already been done in the first set (see Amber Base Trial #5).

Once the desired result is achieved, move on to blending in the next essence in the base accord starting with the higher concentration of the desired base notes and adding smaller amounts of the lesser desired essences.

For example, use Amber Base Trial #9 as the desired result and proceed:

Amber Base	Trial #12	Trial #13
van/lab/styrax (Trial #10)	9 drops	8 drops
beeswax	1 drop	2 drops

Amber Base Trial #13 is the favorite and there are no more

essences to add in, the base note accord for this amber inspired perfume is complete. The reason for not expanding the trials to add in more styrax or beeswax (Amber Base Trial #10 through #13) is because our dominant scent components are the vanilla and cistus formula. If more styrax or beeswax were added, the formulation would be dominant in either of those essences, and the base would not properly reflect the original perfume concept.

Keep good notes on these trials as it may be discovered they are useful in the future. Later inspiration may be gleaned from the 'failed' trials, so be sure to take good notes. To complete the perfume, repeat the trials for the heart/middle accord, and again for the head/top accord.

To blend the three accords together, run more trials, adding together a drop of the base/bottom, a drop of heart/middle and a drop of head/top. If the top notes are too strong, start another trial with two drops base/bottom, two drops heart/middle and one drop head/top. Continue with these trials until the desired result is achieved. Be sure to number the trials and label the trial bottles or scent strips, and keep notes identifying each trial. **The usual ratio of head/heart/base accords is 25% head notes to 20% heart notes to 55% base notes**, though this scale can be adjusted to suit. For example, the head notes may be too dominating in the perfume concentrate, adjust the ratio from 25% to 20% then adjust the heart notes and base notes for a total of 100% of the perfume concentrate (20% head/ 30% heart/ 50% base = 100%).

If at any point in the blending of these accords the perfume has veered in a direction that is not desirable, reformulate to remove or add in another component to the accords. For instance, the head/top accord may not be blending well with the base/bottom accord, find which parts are not working. Based upon the original formula, perform a trial on scent strips with bergamot and the base note (one drop base/bottom accord and one drop bergamot on a scent strip), waft the scent strip to find out if this is the combination that isn't working. Do the same with the coriander. Once it is discovered which element in the head/top note isn't working with the base/bottom note, eliminate it and find another essence in the palette to replace it, or leave it off entirely. It may happen that at the end of these additional trials that the head/top note accord has expanded to include several more individual essences; the same can happen with the heart/middle note accord and base/bottom accord. Blend the three accords and age the finished perfume. Experimentation, evaluation and continued training are the key to better understanding the materials with which a perfumer is working. If a composition ultimately becomes something unfavorable or isn't working, pour the trial into the *Mille Fleurs* bottle and move on to the next formulation project.

To make larger volumes of perfume, convert the drops to milliliters or grams. Follow the instructions in lesson "Drops to Milliliters to Grams" for finding the weight or volume of the trial results, then convert and use the charts in lessons "Milliliters" and "Grams" to make the final solution.

Sacrificial Perfume Materials

Sacrificial perfumery materials are those raw materials which are used to help enhance and improve the fragrance and longevity of another raw material which might otherwise dissipate or disappear into a blend. An example of a sacrificial material might be lemongrass to help enhance and extend the scent-life of lemon or lime essence, or valerian root oil to imitate parts of, and enhance and extend, an oudh. Valerian will also add a slightly sweet, hay-like essence to the product in the dry down, so it may also be used to extend an element in a flouve type perfume (hay absolute). Take into consideration when using sacrificials that they oftentimes can take over a blend if not properly "dosed". Valerian is infamous for its smelly feet essence, a scent which wouldn't necessarily work in perfume. These sacrificial perfume materials are typically used in very small amounts, much less than the essence for which they are being sacrificed, as their scent profiles are oftentimes more intense.

The "Prestige" Note

The word "prestige" today connotes success and achievement. Historically, however, prestige was meant to convey "deceits, delusions," and "juggler's tricks". Basically, magic tricks. In perfumery the prestige note is a magic trick, it changes everything in an otherwise bland, flat, emotionless perfume. For example, a linear honey/floral perfume can be made iridescent and sparkly with the addition of fresh ginger or pink pepper oils, changing the sweet character of the perfume to one with spicy, honeyed wood notes that lift off the skin and seem to breathe like a living creature. Or the prestige note could be a rare raw material, such as *oudh*. The prestige note can be a single raw material or an accord.

Perfume Accord Building Trials Worksheet

Sample Base Accord Building Trial for Amber/Honey Base Accord:

Essence & Trial #	Trial # & Amount	Trial # & Amount	Trial # & Amount
	Trial #1	Trial #2	Trial #3
Vanilla absolute 10%	5 drops	6 drops	7 drops
Beeswax absolute 10%	5 drops	4 drops	3 drops
	Trial #4	Trial #5	Trial #6
Vanilla absolute 10%	8	9	1
Beeswax absolute 10%	2	1	9
	Trial #7	Trial #8	Trial #9
Vanilla absolute 10%	2	3	4
Beeswax absolute 10%	8	7	6

There is no need to complete a trial #10 with this combination as it would be the same as trial #1 (5/5). Of these trials, Trial #8 was our favorite, so we move on to the next part of creating this base accord.

Essence & Trial #	Trial # & Amount	Trial # & Amount	Trial # & Amount
	Trial #10	Trial #11	Trial #12
Trial #8 combination	5 drops	6 drops	7 drops
Siam benzoin 10%	5 drops	4 drops	3 drops
	Trial #13	Trial #14	
Trial #8 combination	8	9	
Siam benzoin 10%	2	1	

These trials can continue by adding labdanum, rose and other elements to create the desired effect. For this trial round, Trial #12 would be combined with the next element of choice.

Composition Lesson #1

Create a heart note accord utilizing the techniques learned thus far:

Inspiration/Journaling
On-paper Outline
Running Trials

Evaluate the accord and write about in the perfumer's notebook. How can it be used in a completed perfume composition, for example, what heart and head notes might compliment this accord, what might be missing from the accord, etc.

Key considerations:

1. Is this accord balanced?

2. Is this accord in synchronicity with the perfumer's notes and inspiration?

3. Has this accord veered from its original path, but is still interesting enough to continue working on it for another project?

Increasing Head Notes for EdT's, EdC's, EdF's & Aftershaves

It will be necessary to increase the percentage of head notes when composing an eau de toilette, eau de cologne, eau fraiche or aftershave. The reason is simple: the volatile top notes will become diluted when water is added, thereby decreasing their diffusivity. Take a look at a typical toilette water formulation which has been made in the past. The formula is dominated by head notes, and less so by heart notes. In *A Woman Beautiful* by Ella Adelia Fletcher, pub. 1899, the formula for Eau de Lisbon Célèbre is written thus:

Oil of Portugal 1 ounce	
Oil of lemon	½ ounce
Oil of rose	½ drachms
Oil of néroli, bigarade	½ drachms
Spirits of wine (rectified)	2 pints

Rectified spirits of wine used in the development of these antiquarian toilette waters were usually around 84% alcohol and 16%

water. A drachm is the archaic spelling for dram, weighs $1/16^{th}$ of an ounce, and 1.77 grams in the US Customary System. The apothecary weight of 1 drachm is $1/8^{th}$ of an ounce and 3.89 grams. It is more likely these antiquarian formulas used apothecary weight as the unit of measure. "Oil of Portugal" is bitter orange peel oil.

When formulation these types of perfumes, you experiment with the increased percentage of head notes in two ways: either formulate the composition with the intention of producing an eau de toilette, eau de cologne, etc., or increase the percentage of head notes *after* completing a perfume composition. It is much simpler, and the results more desirable, to formulate the composition with the perfume grades' intent firmly established prior to formulating the composition.

Adding distilled water for grading an eau de toilette, eau de cologne or an eau de fraiche is a tricky endeavor. Add the perfume concentrate to the alcohol first, blend it, age it, and when ready, slowly add in the distilled water in one milliliter increments or by drops.

The following chart will help to explain how these dilution ratios can be broken down.

Perfume Grade	Alcohol	Distilled Water/Hydrosol	Perfume Composition
Parfum/Extrait	70.00%	0.00%	30.00%
By drops	70 drops	0 drops	30 drops
Eau de Parfum	80.00%	0.00%	20.00%
By drops	80 drops	0 drops	20 drops
Eau de Toilette	87-91%	5.00%	4-8%
By drops	87-91 drops	5 drops	4-8 drops

Eau de Cologne	85-87%	10.00%	3-5%
By drops	85-87 drops	10 drops	3-5 drops
Eau Fraiche	82-84%	15.00%	1-3%
By drops	82-84 drops	15 drops	1-3 drops
Aftershave/Splash	60-62%	37.00%	1-3%
By drops	60-62 drops	37 drops	1-3 drops

Fining or Clarifying a Finished Composition

Fining is a term recently coined by perfumer Alec Lawless as the process by which perfume compositions are clarified with bentonite clay. Winemakers have been using a similar process for hundreds of years, utilizing elements such as ox blood, egg white, seaweed, fish bladders and milk caseins to clarify wine. The process works by binding the proteins in the fining elements with the solids in the wine, separating them from the clear wine and dropping them to the bottom of the barrel, or bottle, in the case of fining/clarifying perfume.

When adding water or hydrosols to a perfume composition, it may become cloudy. It is important to allow the perfume composition and hydro alcoholic solution to settle and mature. Time will eliminate much of the cloudiness, as may an hour or two in an ultrasonic bath. Placing the bottle of solution into the freezer for 24 hours will also help reduce the cloudiness as the more solid elements, the waxes and non-soluable oils, will freeze solid, thus enabling it to be caught in a filter. Filter the blend after maturation (4-6 weeks). A very effective process by which finished perfume compositions, eau de toilettes, eau de colognes, eaux fraiche and aftershaves can be fined and clarified is through the use of diatomaceous earth, or celite. Diatomaceous earth is the fossilized remains of diatoms, a type of hard-shelled algae. It is very soft and powdery and absorbs both oil and water effectively. To use as a filtration aid, place about a quarter teaspoonful of diatomaceous earth directly into a finished composition, and gently shake the bottle. After a few days of settling, and perhaps a trip to the freezer, clarify the composition by pouring it through a couple layers of coffee filter, or through a single laboratory filter. When the results are crystal clear, the perfume is done and ready for bottling. If it is still cloudy, continue to filter until the composition clears.

Another issue to take into consideration is whether to add in emollients to help with the longevity and 'feel' of an aftershave. The recommended emollient is vegetable glycerin. Adjust the water portion to take into account the amount of vegetable glycerin used. For example, our sample above demonstrates a drop ratio of 60-62 drops of alcohol to 37 drops of distilled water, so we would need to adjust the water portion to a lower percentage to allow for the use of the glycerin ~ 60 – 62 drops alcohol to 32 drops of distilled water to 5 drops of vegetable glycerin to 1 – 3 drops perfume concentrate.

Finishing the Composition

Ageing or maturation is required to achieve the smooth, finished effect of the perfume. Four to six weeks are sufficient to determine if the perfume is a success or a failure. Speed the process by utilizing an ultrasonic device. Some Natural Botanical Perfumers have been known to age their compositions for a year or more to reach the stage of completion.

**See "Ultrasonic Maturation"

Custom Perfumes

Let's say a perfumer has a client who wishes to contract a custom perfume, either for them self or for someone else. Ask a few key questions pertaining to the client's tastes, or the tastes of the person for whom the perfume is being commissioned (what perfumes do they currently use, favorite perfume family, favorite colors, etc.), and the client, through their answers, can provide the perfumer with a general outline of how they want the perfume to turn out, which can be a physical manifestation (perfume) of an intangible –a sunrise; a sunset; a car with the top down, rolling through country roads with the scent of _____ filling the air; their beloved father's tweed jacket; summer sun beating down on a wet sidewalk with steam rising and buses rushing past; mimosa trees blooming in front of grandmother's house where sweet iced tea is greedily gulped by thirsty children rocking lazily in a porch swing; roses in huddled bundles chilling in a florist's refrigerator.

A Brief

In the perfume world, a brief is created by the client, given to the perfume house, who then passes the brief to several of their in-house perfumers (a panel) to begin the work. Within a few weeks, sometimes days, the creations of each in-house perfumer are presented to the client. The client then chooses which of the perfumes most closely resembles their concept, makes some adjustments to the brief and solidifies the concept. Then the perfume, and the updated brief, is given back to the perfumer who created it to expand upon. This process can take weeks to complete, and during this time the concept/brief can be changed time and again until the perfect match of brief and perfume are achieved. Unfortunately, this could mean that after months of hard work on the part of a single perfumer, the client can choose (and sometimes does) a perfume which was created in the beginning stages of the process by a completely different perfumer.

Some perfume briefs can be obscure, nonsensical and elusive. The task of the perfumer is to find a way to turn *anything* described in a brief into a perfume.

A Natural Botanical Perfumer creates a brief in the same way, with a few exceptions: a NBP may not work for a big perfume house, or be in a panel. A NBP works independently and more personally with the client to create the perfume. The time frame for completion of the perfume may well mirror the modern synthetic perfume panel's time frame.

Creating Perfume from a Creative Brief ~ Composition Lesson #2

"I carry your heart with me (I carry it in my heart)
I am never without it (anywhere I go you go, my dear,
and whatever is done by only me is your doing, my
darling)

I fear no fate (for you are my fate, my sweet)
I want no world (for beautiful you are in my world, my true)
and it's you are whatever a moon has always meant
and whatever a sun will always sing is you

(here is the deepest secret nobody knows
here is the root of the root and the bud of the bud and the sky
of the sky of a tree called life which grows higher than the
soul can hope or mind can hide)

and this is the wonder that's keeping the stars apart

I carry your heart with me (I carry it in my heart)"
ee cummings

Creating Perfume from a Merchandising Brief ~ Composition Lesson #3

Create a perfume outline (do not actually formulate the perfume) utilizing a merchandising brief as follows:

o   Target market is 18-25 year old women

- Must embody active, sporty and healthy lifestyles
- Celebrity endorsing perfume is Jennifer Alcorn
- Celebrity endorsement must fit the target market

This is a rather simplified brief as most merchandising briefs include bottle sizes and shapes, box packaging, labeling options, color options, and price options. The only wild card in the brief is the celebrity herself.

Create a Custom Perfume Utilizing a Reverse Brief Method ~ Composition Lesson #4

Create a custom perfume outline using a reverse brief method – taking what is known about a client and write down the bones of the custom perfume, composing the perfume from a combination of observation, and intuitive skills.

Create Perfume Utilizing Identical Formulations in Differing Menstruum ~ Composition Lesson #5

Create a perfume using the same formulation with different menstruum, one of oil, and the other alcohol. The alcohol-based perfume can be at parfum strength, eau de parfum strength, edt, edc or edf strength, whichever is preferred, but the other, the oil, must be of the same strength. Make the oil-based parfum a solid if desired.

Remember to dilute the raw materials in the appropriate menstruum for each experiment.

5 drops patchouli 10%
2 drops cistus 10%
1 drop frankincense 10%
2 drops rose may 10%
2 drops Bulgarian rose 10%

~ 131 ~

2 drops ylang-ylang 10%
3 drops ho wood 10%
3 drops geranium 10%
5 drops pink grapefruit 10%

Formulate both, wait a few days for the formulas to mature (use an ultrasonic), and fill in the Compare/Contrast report which follows:

Form/Time	Alcohol	Oil	Comments
From bottle or container			
On scent strip			
On skin			
1 hour			
3 hours			

8+hours			

What Makes A Perfume *Good?*

There are a few key characteristics to look for when evaluating finished compositions which will tell whether the composition is *good* (remember, good is subjective and tastes vary, but any perfumista can tell a poorly constructed perfume from a beautifully constructed perfume). The first key characteristic *is the composition balanced?* Do all the elements within the compositions, the single notes and accords, meld to create a new scent, or does one stand out and dominate, creating an imbalance? The second key characteristic to consider is *does this composition present complexity?* Does the scent intrigue you? Does it draw you in? The third key characteristic *is the composition harmonious?* Do the elements within the composition work together? The fourth key characteristic is *does this composition offer a surprise?* Do you find yourself coming back for a sniff? Do you find yourself in an "ah ha" moment, intrigued by the use of an element within the composition that you ordinarily would have thought wouldn't work out so well? And the fifth key characteristic is *does this composition have tenacity?* Of the five, the fifth is of least importance as the usual nature of a Natural Botanical Perfume is to dissipate and disappear in a few hours rather than linger on the skin for days. To evaluate a finished composition (this is the end-product, the diluted to grade and matured composition), follow the same steps as in the essence evaluations.

Other Methods of Expanding Olfactory Knowledge

There are other very simple ways in which to expand the perfumer's olfactory knowledge. Take a wine appreciation course, or an ethnic cooking class, particularly East Indian cooking courses. Find something that will focus and hone your skills as a "nose". We subconsciously smell things in the air on a daily basis with literally millions of olfactory pings sending us information about our surroundings – whether the lasagna's burning or the trash needs to be taken out or the baby's diaper needs changing, or the less obvious, insidious scent of musty furnishings which simply send the message "old" to our brains without consciously registering the moldy smell. Smelling on purpose is work.

Consciously smell. When walking into a building, sniff the air. Don't allow the pleasant scents sometimes pumped through air ducts deter you from the mission – sniff the air, consciously acknowledge the air freshener and search the air for other smells; perfume, body odor, unwashed clothing, dirty carpets, cleaning materials, food. Smell for it all. Register it. Remember it. By making conscious smelling a habit, you will find your abilities as a nose expanding.

Suggested Raw Materials to Fill Your Palette

Head/Top Notes: *orange essence oil; *lemon essence oil, *lime essence oil, **bergamot BF, blood orange, mandarin, grapefruit, both pink and white, petit grain, lemony frankincense, violet leaf absolute, fresh ginger, ho wood, sweet fennel, geranium, coriander seed, coriander leaf, black, white and pink pepper, clary sage, palmarosa, petit grain(s), galbanum, lavender

Heart/Middle Notes: jasmine grandiflorum absolute, jasmine sambac, jasmine auriculatum, cananga or ylang-ylang extra, rose damascene absolute, neroli, clove bud, myrrh, galbanum, tuberose, cassia, cassie, nutmeg, cardamom, cinnamon leaf, lavender absolute, rose de mai, tea rose, rose otto, lotus, jonquil

Base/Bottom Notes: patchouli essential oil and/or patchouli absolute, vetiver, labdanum absolute, frankincense (all varieties), Himalayan cedar wood, vanilla absolute, tobacco absolute, cepes/mushroom, ambrette seed, cedar woods, sandalwood (Australian or Vanuatu varieties), fir, spruce, pine, cedar woods, oudh

Essence oils are distilled from the whole fruit of the citrus. Cold-pressed citrus peel oils are phototoxic.
**Bergamot BF ~ Bergaptene free bergamot has been redistilled to remove the chemical which causes phototoxicity.*

When placing new orders, try to include at least one aromatic for each part of a perfume; for example, include at least one head/top note aromatic, one heart/middle note aromatic and one bottom/base note aromatic in the order. Remember to dilute and evaluate each new material as it is received.

Collect vintage and antique oils wherever possible, and purchase the same raw material from several growing areas and individual sources and evaluate them thoroughly. It is the only way to discover which growers produce the raw materials preferred, and which suppliers can provide them.

Branding & Selling Your Perfumes

Branding is defined as a "name, term, sign, symbol or design, or a combination of them intended to identify the goods and services of one seller or group of sellers and to differentiate them from those of other sellers," according to the American Marketing Association (AMA).

So, what does that mean? It means that branding isn't just about getting your perfumes under the noses of your target market, it is, according to Laura Lake, author of the article *"What is Branding and How Important is it to Your Marketing Strategy?"* It is about getting your target market to choose your perfumes over all your competition. According to Lake, the objectives to branding are delivering a message concisely and clearly; that the message confirms your credibility; that it connects with your target market on an emotional level; that it must motivate people to buy your perfumes, and it solidifies a loyal base of clientele.

How is this done? Let's start with the first objective, delivering a concise message. First know what your message is about. As an example of a very concise message, we will look at *Smell Bent, Perfume for Cool People* (www.smellbent.com). "Perfume for cool people," is perhaps one of the bravest, and certainly one of the clearest, examples of a branding message. What they are telling you is that you should buy their perfume because if you're not already cool, their perfume will *make* you cool, and if you are already cool, buying their perfume confirms the fact, and that's cool with them. *Smell Bent*'s brand appears not to take itself too seriously, and that's a serious marketing strategy. They're too cool to care. Their website is funky and splashy, high-lighted by hand drawings of mushrooms, surprised-looking snails and lumberjack werewolves. Clicking on the "order" button takes you to a page with the invitation, "So, you want to buy something, huh? That's cool with us." Cool. There's so much fun going on with this brand, a visitor to their website would be hard pressed to walk away empty-handed.

How does your brand confirm your credibility? Let's stick with our example above. *Smell Bent* confirms their credibility by never breaking form. They stay consistent with their message throughout the sales pitch. On their limited editions page, they explain, *"now you see 'em and now you don't these little buggers are elusive, hanging around for a little bit, but never quite long enough for you to get sick of them it does break our heart that they have to leave, but then again, they say absinthe makes the heart grow fonder. Wait, that's not it ... but you get the point."* Again, we get the "it's all cool" vibe from that statement, but with a little information – the limited editions aren't going to be around long so you had better get them while you can.

How to connect to your target market: This brand's target market is clear – young people, 18 to 25 years of age, who don't have a lot of money to spend on high end niche perfumes, and people who are *cool*, or – at least people who think they're cool. The most expensive item on *Smell Bent*'s website is $20 USD for an 8 ml bottle of perfume. They're so cool, they use Paypal to accept payment! No fussy shopping cart for these guys. This fuss-free image is all over *Smell Bent*'s website. There aren't a lot of pages with extensive written descriptions of their perfumes. For example, click on "scents" and you're directed to a page with a Twister-esque spin board with the words "edt spray exclusives" in the blue circle, "custom bent" in the green, "limited edition" in the yellow, "leisure cruise" in the purple, "classic characters" in the blue, and a question mark in the red. Click the blue circle and you get a page with the first perfume listed as "Blimey, Limey" and a hand drawing of a peg-legged pirate, the scent descriptor for the perfume beginning, "why are pirates pirates? Because they arrrrrrr!", and goes on with, "fresh lime juice taken with a shaker of sugar, made to walk the plank and then splashed into a salty musk . . . nice smellin' indeed, Cap'n!" Not a lot of information about the scent of this perfume to go on, but it's fun! And it's only $20!

How does *Smell Bent* motivate buyers and connect to their clientele on an emotional level? By making them *feel good* every time they visit their website. By ingraining into their brains how cool their perfumes are, how cool buyers are by choosing this brand of perfume over the others, and this is also how *Smell Bent* builds customer loyalty. By being consistently stress-free and offering humor as a balm, delivering a good product at a fair price, and keeping things cool.

Here are a few more examples of NBP's who have created easily recognizable brands:

Ayala Moriel ~ A "sensual aromatic experience", Ayala Moriel offers a wide range of Natural Botanical Perfume options, with over 30 perfumes in her arsenal. Her bottling aesthetic is simple: small tear drop bottles with glass stoppers, simple glass roll-on bottles, and small 5 ml glass screw top bottles. She also offers a wide range of products – Single Natural Botanical Perfumes, Scent Wardrobes, pendants, poison rings, solid perfumes in pill boxes, bath and body care, candles, bespoke perfumes, gift cards, gift sets, refills, samples, teas and elixirs, truffles, workshops and NBP courses. Her website is simple, easy to maneuver and full of information. Her logo is a simple stick figure faerie by which her perfumes are recognized.

Laurie Stern ~Velvet & Sweet Pea's Purrfumery, a clear example of hedonistic pleasantness. The aesthetic is a lush portrayal of Victorian era opulence. Laurie incorporates her love of cats into her business model, utilizing Victorian greeting cards with kittens and cats as her option for labeling. She also uses top drawer packaging, lovely Chanel style Brosse bottles, and bejeweled pill boxes for solid perfumes. Laurie's product offerings include liquid perfume, crème perfume, "Kittylicious Eau de Parfum", cologne, limited editions, face and body whipped frostings and oils, home spa products, hydrosols, seasonal offerings, samples and gift vouchers. Laurie's logo is a picture of her two cats, Velvet and Sweet Pea wearing crowns and enclosed in a vintage style Victorian perfumery label.

Isabelle Gelle~Les Parfums d'Isabelle's website is standard paint-by-numbers; very straight forward, no bells and whistles, no frills and chills. Her perfume packaging aesthetic is a bit more impressive, with an eco-friendly twist. Simple bottles with lovely labels, luxuriously wrapped and beribboned boxes, a wide selection of products and beautifully written perfume descriptions are what really stand out with this perfumer. Part of her aesthetic is recreating historical perfumes from the 1795 to 1805 era. She offers a variety of products – eau de parfum, extraits, eau de toilettes, workshops and courses, perfumed events, and bespoke perfumes. Isabelle's logo is a lovely vintage style   label with her name, Isabelle Gelle Parfum.

Perfume aesthetics run the gamut from simple bottles, simple labeling and limited numbers of products, to the heavily done-up, with fussy labels and ribbons and dozens of products. Gothic to Victorian, Egyptian to witchy, and each perfumer of any success has developed an aesthetic, and brand, that is easily recognized at a glance. Your job is to find what brand/aesthetic suits you and build your perfume empire.

Doing Business

Send out press releases when you're ready to open shop. Online press release companies provide free press release services, getting your brand and information to a wider audience. Start with www.i-newswire.com. Send a press release to your local newspaper or local about-your-town magazines. Advertise in local magazines when you're ready to host a scent event, workshop or perfume exhibition. If you've got the gumption, send a press release and press kit to the New York Times. Get reviews. There are dozens of Natural Botanical Perfume reviewers on the internet, bloggers with followers who both make and use Natural Botanical Perfume.

Selling

You've done all the work; you've learned Natural Botanical Perfumery in a few years of study, conceptualized your brand, printed the marketing materials, labels, business cards, created a newsletter, built a fabulous web site, launched your first few perfumes and advertised until your eyes cross and . . . *nothing happens.* The droves you were anticipating, the web contacts, all the people leaving "You go for it!" messages on your social sites, the relatives and personal friends to whom you chattered on incessantly about your business, not one of them shows up at your web site's doorway. Nobody is buying your perfumes! What do you do now?

You go to the public.

Showcases, workshops and lectures are in order. Contact local gift shops and high end spas in and around your town and schedule a showcase (or exposition). What is a showcase? A showcase is where you display your perfumes and your perfume concept to its best advantage. A table setting for a showcase would include all of your marketing materials; flyers, brochures, business cards and samples, as well as prominently displayed full size bottles of your perfumes. If you make other products such as soap and body oils, display those as well, making sure to place the products which you feel define your business most accurately in a place of honor, like in your hand and under the noses of your prospective clients. Offer beautifully printed discount coupons for first-time customers, and ask them to sign a newsletter sign-up sheet so they can be informed when a new product is released, where your next showcase will be scheduled, or where you will be conducting future workshops and lectures. You cannot rely on your web site alone to "get the word out" as most people live busy, hectic lives and don't have the time to keep up with you. It's your job to keep them apprised through regular contact.

Another venue in which to schedule a showcase is a local winery. If you use organic grape alcohol in your perfumes, a winery is a perfect setting for discussing both perfume and wine and their close associations.

What do you talk about at a showcase? You showcase you – your perfumes and your other natural products and nothing else. Not politics, not religion, not news, just perfume and how you learned it, created it and how it would benefit them, your potential clients, to purchase and use it. Go prepared. Know your materials, the actual essential oils, absolutes and other raw materials used in your perfumes. Educate yourself with a little perfume history. Talk about the differences between Natural Botanical Perfumes and modern synthetic perfumes, the pros and cons. Be honest. Creating a fantasy is part of the allure of perfume, but don't stretch the truth or attempt to portray you as some sort of modern age alchemist. Be you. Be the passionate-about-perfume you.

Workshops are another way to bring the word of Natural Botanical Perfume to your neighbors. Workshops can be either elaborate affairs with 20 or more participants, or simple backyard garden soirees with four or five attendees. The price for admission into your workshop should be determined based on two facts: What the market in your area will bear, and what price you apply to your expertise. If you underprice your workshops you may appear unsure or insecure in your abilities to teach or conduct a successful workshop. If you overprice it, no one will sign up. The best way to find future workshop attendees is through a showcase event. The attendees signing up for a workshop who have already been honored with a showcase already know what you're worth, so it's important to put on a really great showcase. What happens at a workshop? Well, you teach. You teach perfumery your way. What you know. How you learned and how you create your products. You are allowed to hold tight to your secrets yet give enough information that the workshop attendee is able to create perfumes on their own. Again, ask the attendees to sign up for your newsletter, and more importantly, make sure they leave the event feeling as if they've learned something valuable.

Workshops can be scheduled at your church, at a local shop or store, a spa, winery, in a rented space if you're expecting a large number of attendees, or in a beautiful garden.

Lectures can be conducted practically anywhere a large number of people can attend. Your church, again, is a good space to lecture. Contact a local high school or community college art teacher and pitch your lecture. Many will be open to the idea of presenting their students with the concept of perfume as art. Not only will you be opening young minds to new possibilities, you may also be looking into the faces of your future apprentices. Art Hops are also great places to lecture and showcase your perfumes. Nearly every city has an art council, contact them to schedule an event. The possibilities for creating your own perfumed environment beyond the four walls of your studio are endless when utilizing these few tips.

Your Perfume Story

Every perfumer has a story. Your story begins with the moment you realized there was something special about scent and perfume, and continues with learning as much about the artistry and process of creating perfume. To some clients, it is important that they feel a personal connection with their perfumer (you), so developing, not making up, a perfume story that includes you as the main character is vital to making that connection.

INDEX

~ 142 ~

Glossary of Terminology

Absolute ~ strongly scented material extracted by alcohol or solvent from concrete (see concrete)

Accord ~ (see Chord) musical reference relating to a chord; usually two or more essences combined to create a scent with its own character and distinctive scent; harmonization and balance within a blend of essences

Adulteration ~ also called 'extending' or 'sophisticating' an oil; when materials either natural or synthetic, are added to extend an oil to gain higher profits, or to perfect or sophisticate a poor grade oil to create an illusion of a higher grade oil in an attempt to render it marketable

Alcohol ~ perfume medium, diluent, solvent or carrier (ethanol) for a perfume composition; in natural perfumery, 190 proof organic grape or grain alcohol is preferred (90-95% alcohol content)

Alcohol, denatured ~ a non-potable alcohol; alcohol with a toxic additive which renders the alcohol undrinkable; used in perfumery (not necessarily Natural Botanical Perfumery)

Alcohol, undenatured ~ for use in perfumery, undenatured alcohol refers to alcohol (ethanol/ETOH) which has not been rendered undrinkable through the inclusion of a toxic substance which 'denatures' the alcohol

Aldehyde/Aldehydic ~ refers to a specific set of synthetic fragrance compounds that give a perfume composition lift and effervescence; in natural perfumery, it relates to the lift and sparkle of the top notes, most notably citrus and spices

Amber ~ warm, powdery note in a perfume composition obtained through the combination of styrax benzoin, labdanum, vanilla and other similar aromatic oils

Animalic ~ usually refers to fecal, leathery and fur-like scents, such as hyraceum (hyrax/Africa Stone), ambergris, costus, nargarmotha, patchouli, choya loban, deer musk and civet; can have some connection to indolic botanical materials such as jasmine

Anosmia ~ the inability to smell, OR the inability to smell certain molecules, such as musks

Aromatic ~ strongly scented materials; specifically refers to rich, balsamic essences, but can be used to refer to nearly any deliciously scented botanical material

Attar ~ co-distillation of sandalwood oil with flowers or flowers steam distilled into a receiver containing sandalwood oil

Balance ~ occurs when all three parts (top/head, middle/heart & bottom/base) of a perfume composition are perfectly balanced so that one does not dominate the others

Balsam ~ sweet, warm, woody, resinous materials; exudates of trees (sap)

Balsamic ~ refers to sweet, warm, woody, rich notes such as tolu balsam and benzoin

Base Notes (see Bottom Notes) ~ notes within a perfume composition which are more tenacious and long-lasting; the last notes detected in the dry down of a perfume composition

Base ~ a base is a composition which include head, heart and base note components that are used as a single scenting element; for example, a jonquil base that will be used as a jonquil note in a perfume concentrate is formulated by blending sandalwood, jasmine sambac, orange blossom, tuberose, lime and vanilla; amber is a base composed with the raw materials benzoin, vanilla and labdanum; OR an unscented, unaltered basic component of a product, such as an oil base, lotion base, shampoo base, conditioner base, etc.

Body ~ a well-rounded composition

Bottom Notes ~ (see Base Notes)

Bouquet ~ refers to a blend of flower essences; used more often in pre-modern perfumery to describe rich floral compositions

Brief ~ a perfume blue print; the perfume concept; it usually utilizes descriptors which are not related to scent or perfume, but evoke emotion; for example, the *feeling* of a winter sun rising over a mountain covered in leaf-barren dogwood

Butaflor ~ butane extraction method

Camphoraceous ~ medicinal note found in lavender and rosemary; camphor-like essences such as eucalyptus and tea tree

Carrier Oil ~ oil used as a base or diluent in oil-based and solid perfume making; typically jojoba and fractionated coconut oils due to their longer shelf lives

Chord ~ (see Accord) refers to a combination of two (usually three) or more aromatics to create a single 'essence', or an accord

Chypre ~ (pronounced *shee-prah*) a perfume formulation characterized by bergamot and oak moss rounded off with rich woody essences like patchouli and ambriene

Citrus Notes ~ the notes obtained through the use of citrus; orange, lemon, lime, bergamot, grapefruit, yuzu, lemongrass

Clarifying ~ filtering a finished perfume composition to create a crystal clear result

Classic ~ a scent which follows a perfumery template utilizing a higher percentage of floral notes to create an essence with timeless appeal

Cloying ~ sweet, heavy, almost suffocating and clingy

CO_2 Extraction ~ carbon dioxide extractions, supercritical carbon dioxide extracts; solvent extraction utilizing CO_2 at low temperature and high pressure to create a fragrant product

Coconut Oil, Fractionated ~ a fraction of whole coconut oil (long chain triglycerides are removed); a completely saturated fat that is more stable and has a longer shelf-life than regular coconut oil; used as a menstruum or medium in perfume making

Cologne ~ an essence composition utilizing primarily citrus oils and a high percentage of water; 3 – 5% perfume composition to alcohol and distilled water

Composition ~ concentrated perfume formula

Compound ~ a blend of two or more essences which comprise parts of a composition

Concentrate ~ (see composition)

Concrete ~ solvent extracted waxy substance obtained from botanical materials

Destructive Distillation ~ distillation of materials, seashells, woods or resins, which are intentionally burned, resulting in a material with a smoky, leathery bouquet

Diluent ~ a substance used to dilute

Distillate ~ results of distillation

Distillation ~ separation of the oil compounds within a botanical material through the use of heated water (see steam distillation, hydro distillation and destructive distillation)

Dry Down ~ the final stage of a perfume's life on the skin; base/bottom notes which have the most tenacity within a perfume composition

Eau de Cologne (edc) (*oh du coh-lohn-yu*) ~ same as Cologne; an essence composition utilizing primarily citrus oils and a high percentage of water; 3 – 5% perfume composition to alcohol and distilled water

Eau Fraiche (edf) (*oh fraysh*) ~ "fresh water" contains 1 to 3% perfume composition to alcohol and water

Eau de Parfum (edp) (*oh du pah-fyah*) ~ 8 – 15% perfume composition blend to alcohol; sometimes incorporates less than 5% distilled water or floral hydrosol; second highest concentration of scent to diluent in perfume making

Eau de Toilette (edt) (*oh du twah-let*) ~ 4 to 8% composition blend to alcohol; incorporates a small percentage of distilled water or floral hydrosol; most common concentration in modern perfume making

Earthy Notes ~ refers to notes typified by mossy, moldy, dirty scents, such as patchouli, cepes (mushroom), tree mosses and vetyver

Enfleurage (*ahn-floo-yahj*) ~ ancient method of obtaining scent by repeatedly placing, removing and replacing fragrant botanical materials on sheets of glass that have been glazed with fat (typically cleaned animal fat) to produce a pomade (see pomade)

Essence ~ fragrant raw materials

Essential Oil ~ aromatic material obtained from botanicals through the process of distillation or cold-pressing/expression

Expression ~ method of obtaining an aromatic material (essential oil) through the use of presses which squeeze out the volatile oils of plant materials, typically citrus peels

Extrait ~ highest concentration of scent to diluents in perfume making; 15 to 40% (sometimes up to 50% or 60%) composition blend to alcohol or diluents

Fining ~ term coined by perfumer Alec Lawless, defined as clarifying or clearing a finished perfume by use of bentonite clay, formerly and currently used as a term defining the clarifying of wine

Fixative ~ raw materials or other natural materials which are used in very small amounts (1 to 3%) to help sustain a perfume, holding it down onto the skin so the scent lasts longer; includes distilled water, floral hydrosols, resin and wood tinctures, styrax benzoin and vegetable glycerin

Flat Note ~ a note with no lift or body

Floral ~ flower based composition

Fougere ~ (pronounced *foo-zhayr*) any ferny, mossy scent with lavender at its heart; usually includes patchouli, labdanum, vanilla, tonka and benzoin

Fresh ~ typified by light and airy notes found in green and citrus essences such as galbanum, violet leaf, lemon, lime, grapefruit, bergamot

Fruity ~ fruit essences, usually does not include citrus oils; some examples of fruity essences are davana, magnolia, black currant bud, Roman chamomile; some fruit essences can be obtained through the use of tinctures of fruit such as fig, dried currant, and berries

Green ~ fresh scent of cut grass or fresh leaves; violet leaf absolute is a green note with a green cucumber-like scent; cardamom typifies a spicy/green note; coriander is a classic green note

Gums ~ sticky, resinous substances; plant sap exudates; balsams can also be called gums

Herbal/Herbaceous ~ typified by green and somewhat camphoraceous scents in combination; lavender, rosemary, sages and mints are common herbal essences

Harsh ~ pungent or chemical character within a perfume composition

Hay ~ an essence typified by a coumarin character; tonka, lavender absolute, liatris

Head Note ~ the first notes you smell in a perfume; they're the opening note, the lead or hook note; relatively fleeting, usually lasting no more than 10 or 20 minutes

Heady ~ intoxicating, stimulating or narcotic

Heart Note ~ notes which normally classify or identify the perfume family or theme of the composition; for instance, if your theme is a white floral, then you would blend some combination of jasmine, neroli, tuberose, gardenia tinctures and other 'white' flower oils as the main component of this note

Heavy ~ intense and oftentimes cloying note

Honey ~ sweet, syrupy note

Hydro Alcohol ~ water and 90- 95% alcohol; used in formulating edt's, edc's and edf's

Incense ~ notes incorporating sweet, powdery and resinous essences

Infusion ~ whole botanical materials immersed in a hot medium, diluents or carrier; botanical material in warmed oil is considered an infusion

Ipsilateral ~ affecting the same side of the body (pertains to left/right nostril evaluation)

Isolate (Natural) ~ individual chemical constituents of an essential oil which are fractionally distilled to obtain, or isolate, from the remainder of the chemicals; examples: eugenol, citronellol, linalool

Insoluble ~ raw materials (essential oils, resins, absolutes, concretes, etc.) which do not dissolve in a diluent (alcohol, solvent, oil, water, etc.)

Jojoba ~ *simmondsia californica/ simmondsia chinensis* plant seed wax used as a menstruum or medium in perfume making (also called goat nut)

Leitmotif ~ theme of the perfume composition

Menstruum ~ a solvent

Middle Note ~ (see Heart Note)

Mossy ~ typified by oak moss, tree mosses and accords

reminiscent of forest floor

Narcotic ~ intense and intoxicating essences such as rose, jasmine, hyacinth, gardenia, narcissus and other rich florals (due to indole and/or skatole)

Note/Notes ~ refers to the melody within the composition, the song of the perfume, the theme, or to a particular part of a perfume or an individual essence, or it refers to how the composition is perceived, i.e. 'floral notes', 'woody notes', 'green notes'

œillet ~ French for carnation; clove pink, spicy carnation essence

Olfactory ~ relating to the sense of smell

Organ ~ system of storing bottles of perfume making materials typified by stepped shelving

Organic (oil) ~ oil sourced from plants on which herbicides and pesticides have not been used

Organoleptic ~ capable of being perceived by a sensory organ

Oriental ~ typified by 'amber' and spice notes

Otto ~ rose(s) steam distilled, Turkish or Bulgarian varieties: rose otto

Palette ~ collection of raw materials used by the perfumer to create perfume

Parfum/Perfume ~ (see Extrait)

Perfumer ~ an artist who creates perfume

Pomade ~ fatty substance obtained through enfleurage; the

pomade is then used for solid perfume making, or it is further processed by soaking the pomade in high proof alcohol for several weeks to obtain a fragrant tincture which is filtered and used to make alcohol based perfume

Powdery ~ a note obtained through the blending of sweet, woody notes with fruity, green or citrus notes; typified by the use of vanilla, patchouli, benzoin, labdanum, cananga/ylang-ylang, rose, sandalwood and/or bergamot

Quenching ~ a phenomenon in which it is believed some sensitizing chemicals can be rendered safe (quenched) for skin contact by adding a quenching agent

Raw Material ~ botanical or animal based material used in perfumery; essential oils, absolutes, tinctures, infusions, concretes, pomades, CO2 extractions, dry botanicals, flower petals, etc. are all examples of a raw material

Reconstituted (oil) ~ an identical to nature oil formulated with the use of synthetics to appear as the authentic oil by odor and analysis

Resinoids ~ (see Balsam and Gums)

Sillage ~ (pronounced *see-yahj*) scent left in the wake of the perfume wearer

Soluble ~ raw materials (essential oils, resins, absolutes, concretes, etc.) which dissolve in diluents (alcohol, solvent, oil, water, etc.)

Solvents ~ fluid materials used to dissolve and extract volatile elements of botanicals (water, alcohol, hexane, oil, etc.)

Specific gravity ~ the density of a substance, raw material, as it compares to the standard density of water

Spicy ~ notes which are typically hot in character, such as clove, pepper and cinnamon

Sweet ~ characterized by taste utilizing essences such as vanilla, honey and warm balsamic notes

Tenacity ~ strength of a scent or note characterized by the length of time it lasts on the skin

Top Note ~ (see Head Note)

Ultrasonic Extraction ~ a method of extracting high grade perfumery materials through the use of an ultrasonic device (jewelry cleaner)

Volatile/Volatility ~ evaporating quickly; rate of evaporation of a raw material

Woody ~ notes related to woods or grasses; cedar wood, sandalwood, patchouli and vetyver are examples of woody

Sources/Bibliography

Websites:

A Method of Creation in Perfumery by Jean Carles, available for printing at

www.perfumersapprentice.com/perfumersworkshop/perfumery_education/carles.html

A Short History of Bathing Before 1601
http://www.gallowglass.org/jadwiga/herbs/baths.html

Absolute Trygve, Trygve Harris, Enfleurage of New York City
http://www.absolutetrygve.blogspot.com

The Ancient Art of Perfumery by John H. Snively, a reprint of an illustrated article originally appearing in Harper's Magazine, US, in 1874; reprinted by Wordmax Books, Laurel, MD, USA -- to order a copy of this article (#8079 Preservation Reprint Number) send $7.50 USD via Paypal to wordmaxbooks@comcast.net, plus a flat rate of $2.50 shipping and handling (US only), $5.00 USD shipping and handling (1 copy) (International); include article ID number (#8079) and title (above) in an email or in a Paypal message

Aroma at San Juan Bautista Perfumarie, host ~ Kathryn Degraff www.sjbca.com

The Art of Perfumery by Septimus Piesse, free download here:
http://www.gutenberg.org/etext/16378

Ayala Moriel/Smellyblog http://www.ayalassmellyblog.com

Bihar Times, Killing for Perfume by Maneka Ghadi ~
http://www.bihartimes.com/Maneka/killingforperfume.html

Bo Jensen, website:
http://www.bojensen.net/EssentialOilsEng/EssentialOils.htm

Centre National de la Recherche Scientifique
www.cnrs.fr/

Chery Lin Skin Care, Essential Oil Chemicals, website/PDF file:
http://cherylinskintherapy.co.uk/chemical-constituents-essential-oils-may.pdf

Ebay www.ebay.com

Cosmetics Design.com http://www.cosmeticsdesign.com

The Creative Work of the perfumer at Leffingwell, website:
http://www.leffingwell.com/h&rfragrance/Perfumer.pdf

Dr. Dukie's Phytochemical and ethno botanical Database http://www.ars-grin.gov/duke/

Eden Botanicals, Sandalwood Essential Oil/Mysore Sandalwood Oil
www.edenbotanicals.com/sandalwood-essential-oil.html

Endangered Species
http://www.aknhp.uaa.alaska.edu/zoology/species_ADFG_PDFs/Mammals/sperm_whale_AD
FG_web_060205.pdf

Essential Oil Chemistry at Essential Oil Recipes
www.essential-oil-recipes.com

European Union Cosmetics Directive
http://eurlex.europa.eu/LexUriServ/LexUriServ.do?uri=CONSLEG:1976L0768:20070919:EN:PDF

Fenner's Complete Formulary ~ A Complete Formulary and Handbook, compiled and written
by B. Fenner, 1888, available for printing at:
http://www.swsbm.com/Fenners/Complete%20Formulary-5.pdf

Find the Fragrance to Match Your Mood online article:
http://findarticles.com/p/articles/mi_m0846/is_3_24/ai_n6246653/pg_2
The Good Scents Company
www.thegoodscentscompany.com

History of Perfume at About.com
http://inventors.about.com/llibrary/inventors/blperfume.htm

History of Perfume at Perfumes.com
http://www.perfumes.com/eng/history.htm

History of Perfume at Wikipedia
http://en.wikipedia.org/wiki/History_of_perfume

How to Choose the Right Perfume for Your Body Chemistry
http://www.beauty-and-the-bath.com/How-To-Choose-The-Right-Perfume-For-Your-Body-
Chemistry.html

How to Distill Ethanol or Grain Alcohol at About.com
http://chemistry.about.com/od/chemistryhowtoguide/ht/ethanol.htm

The International Fragrance Association
www.ifraorg.org ~ information booklet at:
        http://www.rifm.org/doc/IFRA%20QRA20%information%20Booklet202008%207%2009%20
43A.pdf

Alexander Lee, J'aime le parfum ~ I love perfume!
http://jaimeleparfum.wordpress.com/

Kitchen Doctor
www.kitchendoctor.com (Four Thieves Remedy, Ingrid Naimen 2004)

MSDS Solutions Center
www.msds.com

My Madeleine blog
http://mollysmadeleine.blogspot.com/200/12/unexpected-scent-of-chocolate.html

Monclin; Homemade monclin instructions:
http://evanizer.com/perfume/monclin/index.html

Musees de Grasse Perfume History
http://www.museesdegrasse.com/MIP/fla_ang/histo_fXIX.shtml

NAHA Opinion Document ~ A Brief Safety Guidance on Essential Oils ~ Tony Burfield
http://naha.org/articles/brief_safety%20guidance%2-.htm

National Geographic "Aphrodite's Island"
http://news.nationalgeographic.com/news/2007/03/070329-oldest-perfumes.html

Notes From the Ledge (blog)
http://scelfleah.blogspot.com

Online Conversion
www.onlineconversion.com

Perfumer's Apprentice
www.perfumersapprentice.com

Perfumes in Mediterranean Antiquity
www.interscience.wiley.com DOI 10.1002/ffj.1944

Perfume Shrine Blog
http://perfumeshrine.blogspot.com/2009/11/perfume-use-in-middle-ages-and.html

Precision Weighing Balances
www.balances.com

A Queen's Delight by M.W. free download here:
http://www.gutenbrg.org/etext/15019

Research Institute for Fragrance Materials
www.rifm.org

Scientific Committee on Consumer Products/SCCP

http://ec.europa.eu/health/ph_risk/committees/04_SCCP_opinions_en.htm

Smell & Psychology of Scent online book (pg. 1)
http://books.google.com/books?id=GHt6AlrwNdIC&pg=PA81&dq=scent+evaluation+nostril&source=bl
&ots=KdxQbxSyXu&sig=-
dTK_9teksEQOECu6GBVMILVDQ&hl=en&sa=X&oi=book_result&resnum=9&ct=result

The Smell Report
http://www.sirc.org/publik/smell_emotion.html

Synesthesia, *Wikipedia (online)*

Ultrasonic Extraction & Preservation
http://www.hielscher.com/ultrasonics/extraction_01.htm

Wallach, Otto
http://nobelprize.org/nobel_prizes/chemistry/laureates/1910/press.html

Washington Post
www.washingtonpost.com/wpdyn/content/article/2006/01/30/AR2006013001240.html

Web MD
http://www.webmd.com/allergies/news/20090616/fda-some-zicam-cold-remedies-are-risky

Wine Definitions
http://www.winedefinitions.com/learningcenter/articles/fining.htm

Zicam
http://www.zicam.com/messagetoconsumers

Publications / Lecturers / Personal Contacts:

A Woman Beautiful by Ella Adelia Fletcher, p. 1901

The Alchemy of Hydrosols by Dabney Rose

Aromatherapy for Massage Practitioners by Ingrid Martin, p. 2006, ISBN-10:0781753457;
ISNB-13: 978-0781753454

Aromatherapy: Scent & Psyche, Peter & Kate Damian, Healing Arts Press, 1995

The Art of Perfumery, and Method of Obtaining the Odors of Plants by
G.W. Septimus Piesse (p. 1857)

The Art of Soap Making by Merilyn Mohr, 1996

Artisan Perfumery/Being Led by the Nose by Alec Lawless, p. 2006, ISBN 978-0-9562137-0-9

Blending Booklet by Jeanne Rose

British Society of Perfumers, Speaker: Yuri Gutsatz, Paris, 1999

Carles, J., A Method of Creation in Perfumery, Reserches, 11 Dec. 1961, pp. 8-25; 12 Dec. 1962, pp. 18-29; 13 Dec. 1963, pp. 92-103

Chemistry and Technology of Flavors and Fragrances by David J. Rowe (Editor); Chapter 13: Applications II: Fragrance by Stephen J. Herman

Christine Malcolm, Santa Fe Botanical Fragrances

Clean: An Unsanitised History of Washing, by Katherine Ashenberg, 2008

The Complete Guide to the Use of Oils in Aromatherapy & Herbalism, Julia Lawless, 1995

Cosmetic Recipes The Recipe Book of Mary Doggett, transcribed by Sally Pointer, 2004

Dermatitis, Textbook of Cosmetic, p. 624, Rycroft, Menne, Frosche, Benezra, pub. 1994, ISBN: 354066842X, 9783540668428

De Materia Medica, Dioscoride

Encyclopedia of Practical Receipts & Processes by Dickrich, pub. 1879

Essential Chemistry for Safe Aromatherapy by Sue Clarke, p. 2002, ISBN-10: 0443064857; ISBN-13: 978-0443064852

Essential Oil Safety: A Guide for Health Care Professionals, Tisserand and balac, ISBN: 0443052603

Fragrance History by Mindy Green

France Monthly, May 2006

Frankincense & Myrrh by Martin Watt and Wanda Sellar, p. 1996, ISBN 0 85207 306 2

Gloria O. Hammer, Aromatherapist, Phyto-Aromatherapist & Natural Perfumer

The History of Houbigant Perfumes, Perfume Projects, Lightyears Collection, Lightyears, Inc.

The Illustrated Encyclopedia of Essential Oils by Julia Lawless, pub. 1995, ISBN: 1-55519-990-5

La Dolce Vita Perfume, New Holland Publishers, 2001

Mountain Rose Herbs, Neti Pot

The Nose ~A Profile of Sex, Beauty, and Survival by Gabrielle Glaser, pub. 2002, ISBN: 0-671-03863-X; 0-671-03864-8 (pbk)

Nostradamus: Translation from French from the *Books of Nostradamus,* written in 1552; *The*

Elixirs of Nostradamus, Nostradamus' Original Recipes for Elixirs, Scented Water, Beauty Potions and Sweetmeats, edited by Knut Boeser, 1994

Dr. Oz on Oprah, Spring 2007, demonstrates use of Neti Pot

Plant Aromatic Safety Data by Martin Watt; manual or booklet

Perfume by William Kaufman (p. 1974); Carles, J., *A*

Method of Creation in Perfumery, Reserches, 11 Dec. 1961, pp. 8-25; 12 Dec. 1962, pp. 18-29;13 Dec. 1963, pp. 92-103

Perfume and Flavor Materials of Natural Origin by Steffan Arctander, copyright 1994 by Allured Publishing, ISBN: 0-931710-36-7

Perfume: Joy, Obsession, Scandal, Sin Richard Stamelman, A Cultural History of Fragrance from 1750 to the Present, 2006

Perfumes in Mediterranean Antiquity, Cecilia Castle, Xavier Fernandez, Jean-Jacques Filippi, Jean-Pierre Brun, Abstract, The Seplasia Project, John Wiley & Sons, Ltd., Flavour and Fragrance Journal

Perfume: Story of a Murderer by Patrick Suskind, 1986

Perfumer's Apprentice, Linda Andrews

The Practice of Aromatherapy Dr. Jean Valnet, 2004

Rome on the Euphrates by Freya Stark

Rose, Jeanne, Aromatherapist, Author, NBP interview 2009

Scents of Time, Perfume from Ancient Egypt to the 21ˢᵗ Century, Edwin T. Morris, Metropolitan Museum of Art, 1999

The Secret of Scent ~ Adventures in Perfume and the Science of Smell by Luca Turin, p. 2006, ISBN-10: 0-06-113383-3; ISBN-13: 98-0-06-113383-1

Soap, Perfumery & Cosmetics Buyer's Guide & Cyclopaedia, 1938

Spagyrics by Manfred M. Junius, copyright 1979, ISBN-13: 978-1-58477-179-8; ISBN-10: 1-59477-179-0

Tauer, Andy, Swiss Perfumer, ScentBar, 2008 lecture and perfume sampling; Immersive Sculpture

Theophrastus, On Odours

Turin, Luca, blog (removed) 2005 blogs on Monclin

What the Nose Knows by Avery Gilbert

The World of Aromatherapy by Jeanne Rose and Susan Earle, 1996

Textbook of Contact Dermatitis by Rycroft, Menne, Frosche, Benezra, pg. 624, (pub.1994), ISBN: 354066842X, 9783540668428

Sourcing Raw Materials & Supplies

Alchemical Solutions
> http://www.alcsol.com
> Organic grape and grain alcohol. 866-801-1050

American Science Surplus
> http://www.sciplus.com/
> Flasks, droppers, dropper bottles. No min. Great prices. 888-724-7587, offers paper catalog

Best Bottles
> http://www.bestbottles.com
> Small metal and plastic funnels, 1.26 in. across; fancy perfume bottles 510-487-8000

Freund Container and Supply
> http://www.freundcontainer.com
> Bottles, vials, labels, boxes 800-363-9822

Liberty Natural
> www.libertynatural.com
> $50 minimum order; no tax ID required. 1-800-289-8427

Madina Industrial Corporation
> http://www.madinaonline.com
> Perfume bottles, vials, cobalt/amber bottles, droppers 800-887-2368

Mountain Rose Herbs
> www.mountainroseherbs.com
> Raw materials, organic oils, herbs. No minimum. Great pricing. 800-879-3337 – offers paper catalog

Nature's Gift
> www.naturesgift.com
> No minimum; no tax ID required. Top quality materials. 614-612-4270

New Directions Aromatics
> www.newdirectionsaromatics.com

Orders below $100 are subject to a 10% small order fee. Good prices. 1-800-246-7817

Perfumer's Apprentice
http://www.perfumersapprentice.com
Raw materials, natural perfumery kits, scent strips, glassine envelopes, bottles
1-831-466-0288

Samara Botane
www.wingedseed.com
Raw materials, bottles and jars, books

Scalesonline.com
http://www.scalesonline.com
Scales, scales & more scales! Every price range and weight capability
866-856-6100

Sun Burst Bottle Co.
http://www.sunburstbottle.com/
Perfume bottles, vials, blue cobalt and amber bottles. No min. Great prices. 916-929-4500

Sunrose Aromatics
www.sunrosearomatics.com
No minimum; no tax ID required; lower purchase price for those holding a wholesale or tax ID license. Top quality raw materials. 718-794-0391

ULINE Shipping Supplies Specialists
http://www.uline.com/Index.aspx
Velveteen drawstring bags, packaging boxes, shipping boxes, etc.

White Lotus Aromatics
www.whitelotusaromatics.com
$100 minimum; tax ID required for Washington State residents only. Many aromatics from which to choose. Top quality raw materials. FAX only: 360-457-9235

White Witch
www.whitewitch.ie
No minimum; top quality raw materials; fast shipping; great prices

Suppliers Worldwide

A & E Connock, Inc.
http://www.connock.co.uk/
sales@connock.co.uk
Aromatics, waxes, waters, distillates

Albert Vieille
www.albertvieille.com
info@albertvieille.com
Natural aromatics; absolutes, concretes, CO2 extractions, essential oils, gums, resinoids

Alfa Chem
http://www.alfachem1.com/
alfachem@gmail.com
Natural essential oils, essential oils and resinoids

African Bush Company
http://www.africanbush.com/
info@africanbush.com
Essential oils and botanicals

Artiste Flavor and Essence
http://www.artisteflavoressence.com/
info@artisteflavoressence.com
Citrus products; tea, coffee & cocoa extracts; essential oils & absolutes; infusions and distillates; oleoresins; natural aromatic chemicals; aroma chemicals; flavors & fragrances

Berjé Inc.
www.berjeinc.com
berje@berjeinc.com
Essential oils; aroma chemicals; CO2 extracts/templar oils

Biolandes

http://www.biolandes.com/english/group/
See website for contact information
Raw materials; flavor extracts

Charabot
http://www.charabot.com/
contact@charabot.fr
Raw materials, perfumery school

Essential Oil Company
http://www.essentialoil.com/
Distillation equipment, essential oils

Frutarom
http://www.frutarom.com/
info@frutarom.com
Essential oils, natural extracts, distillates

Grain Processing Corporation
http://www.grainprocessing.com/
sales@grainprocessing.com
Ethyl alcohol
Lebermuth Company
http://www.lebermuth.com/
info@lebermuth.com
Essential oils, botanicals

Moellhausen Spa
http://www.moellhausen.com/
ho@moellhausen.com
Extracts, absolutes, concretes, essential oils, isolates

Natural Sourcing
http://www.naturalsourcing.com/
info@naturalsourcing.com
Essential oils, CO2 extracts

Prima Fleur Botanicals
http://www.primafleur.com/
sales@primafleur.com
Raw materials, extracts, hydrosols, essential oils, absolutes

Robertet

http://www.robertet.com/
fragrances@robertet.fr
Essential oils, absolutes, distillates, fractions

Recommended Reading

Advanced Aromatherapy, The Science of Essential Oil Therapy by Kurt Schnaubelt, Ph.D.

A Natural History of the Senses by Diane Ackerman

Aromatherapy for Massage Practitioners by Ingrid Martin, pub. 2006, ISBN-10: 0781753457; ISBN-13: 978-0781753456

Artisan Perfumery/Being Led by the Nose by Alec Lawless

The Art and Science of Scent ~ Perfume by Cathy Newman

The Art of Perfumery, and Method of Obtaining the Odors of Plants, G.W. Septimus Piesse, published 1857, University of Michigan, University Library currently publishes this work ~ can be purchased through Amazon.com

The Book of Perfume by Elizabeth Barille & Catherine Laroze

Book of Perfumes by Eugene Rimmel, 1865

The Chemistry of Fragrance from Perfumer to Consumer edited by Charles S. Sell

The Chemistry of Fragrances by David H. Pybus & Charles S. Sell

Cosmetics, Fragrances & Flavors: Their Formulation & Preparation by Louis Appell

Essential Chemistry for Safe Aromatherapy by Sue Clarke, pub. 2002, ISBN-10: 0443064857; ISBN-13: 978-0443064852

Essential Oil Safety: A Guide for Health Care Professionals by Tisserand and Balac, ISBN: 0443052603

Fragrance by Edwin T. Morris

The Fragrant Path by Louise Beebe Wilder

The Herbalist by Joseph E. Meyer

The Illustrated Encyclopedia of Essential Oils by Julia Lawless

The Mystery of Perfume by Rita Schnitzer

Perfume by William Kaufman, 1974

Perfume ~ Joy, Obsession, Scandal, Sin: A Cultural History of Fragrance from 1750 to the Present by Richard Stamelman

Perfume Album by Jill Jessee, Original Edition 1951

Perfume and Flavor Materials of Natural Origin by Steffen Arctander, p. 1961; reprint publication by Allured Publishing
The Perfume Guide by Susan Irwin

Perfume Legends; French Feminine Fragrances by Michael Edwards

The Romance of Perfume by Richard le Gallienne

Scents of Time published by Bulfinch Press, from The Metropolitan Museum of Art

The Science and Art of Perfumery by Edward Sagarin

Textbook of Contact Dermatitis by Richard J.G. Rycroft, Torkil Menne, Peter J. Frosch and Claude Benezra

What the Nose Knows by Avery Gilbert

Online Educational Sites, Groups, Research/Reference & Articles

Basenotes ~ http://www.basenotes.net/columnists/20070223cropwatchvsifra.html

Bo Jensen ~ http://www.bojensen.net/

Cropwatch ~ http://www.cropwatch.org

Dead Media ~ http://www.deadmedia.org/notes/6/069.html

Dr. Duke's Phytochemical & Ethnobotanical Databases ~ http://www.ars-grin.gov/duke/

Edmond Roudnitska, Master Perfumer and Feminist Supporter ~ http://www.art-et-parfum.com/roudnitska.htm

Formpak Active ~ http://www.formpak-software.com/active/

The Good Scents Company ~ http://www.thegoodscentscompany.com/

Leffingwell ~ http://www.leffingwell.com/

National Geographic ~ http://news.nationalgeographic.com/news/2007/03/070329-oldest-perfumes.html

Nature's Nexus ~ http://www.naturesnexus.org

Scented Pages ~ http://scentedpages.com

White Lotus Aromatics ~ http://www.whitelotusaromatics.com/newsletters/newsletter.html

Biopiracy:

http://en.wikipedia.org/wiki/Biopiracy

http://www.williams.edu/go/native/biopiracy.htm

http://www.stallman.org/articles/biopiracy.html

Brick & Mortar (US only)

The Perfumer's Apprentice
Upstairs: 1319 Pacific Avenue
Downtown Santa Cruz, CA 95060

Ajne
Corner of Ocean & Dolores
Across the street from Paloosh
Carmel, CA

Secret Gardens Tour
Velvet & Sweetpea's Purrfumery
Laurie Stern, Perfumer
info@purrfumery.com or (510) 528-8040

Persephenie
304 S. Edinburgh Avenue
Los Angeles, CA
(323) 658-7507

Strange Invisible Perfumes
1138 Abbot Kinney Boulevard
Venice, CA
(310) 314-1505